ANUSZKIEWICZ

KARL LUNDE

ANUSZ

KIEWICZ

HARRY N. ABRAMS, INC., PUBLISHERS, NEW YORK

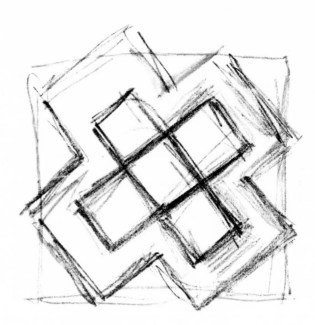

1. Working sketch

Library of Congress Cataloging in Publication Data
Lunde, Karl.
  Richard Anuszkiewicz.
  Bibliography: p.
  Includes index.
  1. Anuszkiewicz, Richard. I. Anuszkiewicz, Richard
ND237.A645L86   759.13   76–28230
ISBN 0–8109–0363–6

Library of Congress Catalogue Card Number: 76–28230
Published in 1977 by Harry N. Abrams, Incorporated, New York
Printed and bound in Japan

CONTENTS

LIST OF ILLUSTRATIONS

Colorplates are marked with an asterisk (*)

The art of Richard Anuszkiewicz is an exploration of color. As he has stated: "The image in my work has always been determined by what I wanted the color to do. Color function becomes my subject matter, and its performance is my painting."[1] For Anuszkiewicz an investigation of color is reason enough for the creation of a painting, and throughout his career he has refined his methods of focusing upon the self-imposed problems that have been his concern.

For this reason he has often been considered a scientific artist. Anuszkiewicz is the first to admit that he is not a scientist, although it is true that he has been profoundly interested in the psychology of visual perception and in the interaction of color. But in his approach to the testing of a color problem in painting he experiments like a laboratory technician, carefully avoiding the imposition of his personality and preconceptions upon it. This becomes apparent in his painting procedure, which is planned, in his impersonal uniform surface, his symmetry, his rejection of the accidental and biographical, his use of repetition, his intellectualism, and his technical discipline.

That his pictures delight the receptive eye is attested by critical comment on recent exhibitions. As long ago as 1967 one reviewer, who called Anuszkiewicz a "master magician of cool pyrotechnics," remarked: "The colors glow and shimmer . . . with a calm, almost classical beauty."[2] Another critic, in 1975, said: "Anuszkiewicz combines vibrantly trans-

2. Anuszkiewicz at work

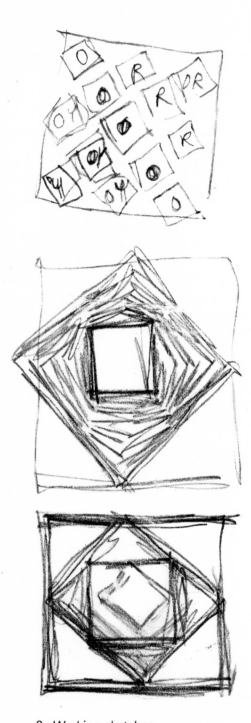

3. Working sketches

fused color, conformity of scheme, and exquisite precision as handsomely as ever. . . . The effect is so to deepen and invigorate [the color] field that it seems to be producing light rather than reflecting it."[3] The seductive colors which have in recent years replaced the more shocking contrasts of the artist's works of the early 1960s (when he was first noticed as an Op art leader) now seem to some observers evocative of delicate tints of the atmosphere, of sunrise, twilight, moonlight, sunset.

His works are now found in major museums and collections; hung in international exhibitions, both one-man and group; and discussed and reproduced in standard art-historical texts and reference books. An understanding of the artist and his present importance can be had by studying the circumstances of his family background and education, the New York art scene in the early 1960s, and especially the integrity of his pursuit of artistic goals.

4. Anuszkiewicz with his wife and their children. Anuszkiewicz's father, Adam, holds one of his own paintings. Painting in background is *Apex*, 1966 (see plate 148).

Richard Anuszkiewicz's father, Adam, was born in a small Polish village in 1890. Because he would have been drafted into the Czar's army at twenty-one, Adam Anuszkiewicz came to the United States at the age of nineteen, settling in Erie, Pennsylvania. There is some irony in the fact that he was drafted into the U.S. Army in 1918, but he became a citizen thereby and never had to serve overseas. He worked for thirty-

5. Anuszkiewicz's mother and sister
Lillian. c. 1928

nine years for a paper mill in Erie, retiring in 1956. He helped his son to build canvas stretchers for large works and became a painter himself, working in a style similar to Richard's.

Anuszkiewicz's mother, Victoria Ann Jankowski, was also born in 1890, in a Polish village located a short distance from the birthplace of his father. Although they grew up near each other, the couple first met in Erie. Victoria had been married at sixteen to a man of thirty-two from her own village; together they had emigrated to Erie, where her husband found work as a laborer. Five children, Richard's half brothers and half sister, followed in rapid succession. In 1923, they all went to Poland to visit and to inspect some property. While there, her husband died, and Victoria, leaving the land holdings untouched, returned to Erie with her children.

For five years the widow supported her family by holding two jobs: cleaning for a doctor during the day and cleaning an office at night. In 1928, when her youngest child was nine and her eldest (who gave his mother away at the wedding) was eighteen, she married Adam Anuszkiewicz, who was a bachelor. Richard, the only child of this union, was born in 1930. His mother died in 1964.

In 1960 Richard Anuszkiewicz married Elizabeth (Sally) Feeney, a sparkling fifth-generation Irish-American girl, whose parents lived in East Orange, New Jersey, and whose mother's grandfather had fought in the American Civil War. Sally, an only child, belongs to the first generation of her family to marry anyone of non-Irish descent. For seven years she was a primary-school teacher, until responsibility to their three children—Adam, Stephanie, and Christine—led to her decision to give up that career.

Since his marriage Anuszkiewicz and his close-knit family

have lived within convenient distance from the New York metropolitan art centers, where his work was then beginning to find public recognition. In 1967 he established his home and his studio in Englewood, New Jersey, just across the Hudson from New York City. Anuszkiewicz, with the cooperation of his wife, has taken part in local activities, both artistic and social, lending a hand to educational, political, and environmental programs and exhibitions of interest to the community or the state. Throughout America he has lectured, demonstrated his art methods and theories, juried shows, and contributed his work to charitable fund raising.

"Artists can't back off and say all they're going to do is their paintings," Anuszkiewicz has said. "They have a responsibility, to society and to the environment."[4]

Superficially, Anuszkiewicz appears to be an uncomplicated, placid person, and certainly he is socially comfortable, relaxed, and direct; but his conversation is highly abstract, and his restlessness and search for variety drive him to pace the floor when he is alone or to jump into his car impulsively and drive for hours. Not only has he a need for variety, but he enjoys all kinds of art and music, people, and experiences. His surface is held in balance like the tense surface of his paintings, and the rearrangement of any part of the highly ordered surface may release the conflicting energies within.

Given his ethnic background, it is tempting to relate Anuszkiewicz's love of bright colors and geometric patterns to his heritage—perhaps to such Polish folk arts as Easter-egg decoration. However, the Anuszkiewicz family had no folk art at home, and Anuszkiewicz does not recall having seen any folk art elsewhere at that time. He seems to be completely a product of his American environment. His first paintings were done in Erie under the guidance of an Impressionist teacher interested in regional Americana, and it was not until his studies with Josef Albers at Yale, during the mid-1950s, that Anuszkiewicz became aware of the possibility of bright color juxtaposition, which he had previously been taught was "wrong."

Anuszkiewicz began doing watercolors—primarily of an architectural nature—in high school. His teacher, Joseph Plavcan, acquainted him with Impressionist color theory, the Ostwald system of complementary colors, and the spectrum prism. The young student was restricted to an Impressionist palette—red, blue, yellow, and their complementaries; black was forbidden.

His paintings during this time were realistic. It was only during his studies in the Cleveland Institute of Art (1948–53), where he received a Bachelor of Fine Arts degree, that he began to simplify landscape and still life into design and abstraction.

Eight Windows of 1951 (plate 8), is a painting in peach, light brown, and green. Here Anuszkiewicz was less interested in the realistic transcription of detail than in the abstraction created by the pattern of asymmetrically arranged tiers of windows.

Shape and arrangement also constitute the crux of the *Six Altar Boys at Sanctus* (1951, plate 7), in which two groups of three boys are separated symmetrically by the partially seen figure of the priest.

He spent an extra year at Cleveland, and during this time his paintings became simpler. *Back Porch* (1952, plate 6) is typical. His paintings from high school and college years, showing derivations from Charles Burchfield and Edward Hopper, were found worthy of awards and received some

6. *Back Porch.* 1952. Oil on canvas,
   36 × 24″. Collection the artist

7. *Six Altar Boys at Sanctus*. 1951. Oil on Masonite, 14 × 34″. Collection the artist

local acclaim. Anuszkiewicz said of this youthful output, "You could call me a sort of Midwest regional painter. In a sense, though, it was related to what I'm doing now [1965]. I painted that way because I was interested in the shapes, not the subjects."[5]

Anuszkiewicz was awarded a Pulitzer scholarship by the National Academy of Design in 1953 and then studied at Yale, receiving a Master of Fine Arts degree in 1955. He worked from the start with Josef Albers, who considered him his best pupil. At Yale he continued to paint realistically but tried many styles; change came painfully and slowly to him.

"I worked in a semiabstract manner," he has said of this

period. "I struggled to preserve what I already had. I only felt liberated after I left."[6]

There are two studies from 1955, however, that are related to his later work in the use of colored line. One is the *Mask* (plate 10), inspired by Paul Klee's *Actor's Mask* of 1925 (plate 11). The strong blue background, the green and red lines, the blue and red bottom are the first marked departure in Anuszkiewicz's work. He became aware of Klee because Albers taught Klee's principles of color. In Germany Klee and Albers both had taught in the Bauhaus, and Albers took over the Bauhaus courses in color from Johannes Itten in 1923, becoming director of that course when the Bauhaus moved from Weimar to Dessau in 1925. When the Nazis closed the Bauhaus in 1933, its teachers were dispersed throughout Europe as well as the United States, giving the Bauhaus an importance it might never have had if it had been confined to Dessau. Albers came to America in 1933 and was a professor at Yale for about ten years from 1950 on. He died in 1976.

The second Anuszkiewicz work, untitled, from 1955 (plate 13) is related to the *Mask* and shows a head with a green border. The inspiration was again Klee. Anuszkiewicz has said, "Klee's conscious involvement with color impressed me a great deal. His borders are particularly beautiful: take for example the 1918 painting *With the Eagle* [plate 12]; here he has brown reds, dirty colors—but with the bright green border, he makes dirty colors warm; they're brought to life. Klee is very perceptive about color. What his paintings 'mean,' the psychological quality, or its revelation of a state of mind or being, doesn't interest me at all—it's purely objective."

Anuszkiewicz learned from Klee that it is not necessary to make big paintings. Klee's works are not large nor obvious or pompous. They are of the size necessary for his ideas.

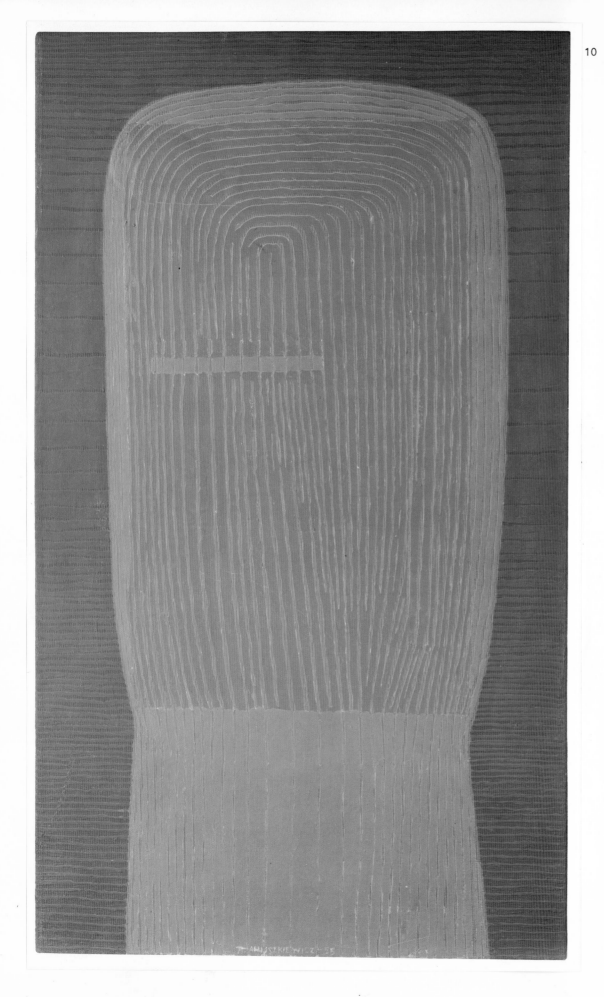

10. *Mask*. 1955. Oil on canvas, 30 × 18″.
Collection the artist

11. Paul Klee. *Actor's Mask*. 1925. Oil on canvas
mounted on board, 14 3/8 × 14 3/8″.
The Museum of Modern Art, New York (Sidney and
Harriet Janis Collection)

12. Paul Klee. *With the Eagle*. 1918. Watercolor on gesso ground,
6 3/4 × 9 3/4″. Kunstmuseum, Bern (Paul Klee Collection)

13. Untitled. 1955. Oil on board,
23 × 19 1/2″. Collection the artist

13

At Yale, Anuszkiewicz attended studio classes and art history classes. Along with general surveys, and such subjects as a history of prints, Anuszkiewicz also sat in on a course in Far Eastern art, and the first art he ever bought for himself was a group of Japanese prints for twenty-five dollars at a book-store. His interest in printmaking was later to bear fruit in his own career, and his admiration for Japanese wood blocks has continued.

Albers's color course at Yale was part lecture and part studio. "It was a two-hour class, and color problems were given at the end of class. Next time they were handed in, and we would talk about them." Then there would be the presentation of new ideas, and work would start on these. Albers had assistants who worked with the students. An example of a color problem might be to find or select pieces of paper that one perceives as white, the question being, "What is white?" By comparing one piece with another the students would discover that there is no such color as white. They would then make free compositions of the different pieces. A more typical color problem might be to make one color look like two different colors or vice versa—a question of finding the right backgrounds. Another might be to make an opaque color look transparent. Albers placed colors next to each other in order to see what would happen, having no preconceived idea as to the result. He presented no color "theory" as such, no set of rules or dicta. Rather, he *used* color; he studied the *relativity* of color.

When asked what Albers had taught him, Anuszkiewicz replied, "A disciplined method of working. He did teach me to look abstractly at a painting. Before working with him, I had difficulty in looking at something objectively."

Two writers whose work Anuszkiewicz studied attentively during his years at Yale were James J. Gibson and Rudolf Arnheim, psychologists concerned with perception. A study of their writings as well as those of other specialists in phenomena of perception led to Anuszkiewicz's choice of subject for his master's thesis in fine arts, "Study in the Creation of Space with Line Drawing." The thesis is a synthesis of current ideas in perception, illustrated with examples of art ranging from the Altamira caves to Picasso. In it Anuszkiewicz said, "Modern art dispensed with many limitations; among the more important was 'clearly defined dominances,' where one object could definitely precede another, or where space was clearly defined." He discussed five ways of creating space—variety of line, overlapping, reduction of detail, perspective, and size. And he concluded: "Through their studies, modern psychologists have presented to us ways of 'seeing' works of art more competently. They have shown to us how the eye organizes visual material according to definite psychological laws. Vision is not a mechanical recorder of elements, but a grasping of structural patterns. The relationship between artist and psychologist has proven a benefit for both. . . . An artist must know the rules before he is validly able to break them."

After Yale, Anuszkiewicz felt a need to pursue his formal education and attended Kent State University in Ohio in 1955–56, receiving a Bachelor of Science degree in education. He had thought of teaching as a supplement to his painting career, and the example of such a master as Albers indicated that the two careers are compatible. Anuszkiewicz did teach later at Cooper Union Art School, in New York City, Dartmouth College (where he was Artist in Residence in 1967), the University of Wisconsin, Cornell, and Kent State (1968), and has continued to give lectures and demonstrations from time to time at other schools.

As a teacher, he stresses principles and ideas rather than method. He believes that the best education for a painter is the greatest possible exposure to all ideas, all kinds of art, and that only through an awareness of the history of art can the artist make a statement that is either personal or relevant to his own time.

During his stay at Kent State in 1955 he was given a one-man exhibition by the Butler Art Institute, Youngstown, Ohio. The pictures he showed there still reflected many of the earlier influences and were, as he thinks of them now, primarily student work but beginning to turn to a direction of his own.

His academic education behind him, Anuszkiewicz moved about, searching for a livelihood, a way to come to grips with his work. He did a stint of house painting, tried his luck in New York, where he found a job repairing models of classical temples at the Metropolitan Museum of Art, and then traveled off to see for himself the wealth of art and architecture in northern Africa and western Europe.

On his return, his efforts to have his paintings exhibited in New York went unrewarded until 1960, when his first one-man show in the city was presented by The Contemporaries.[7] It was a fully-developed statement, going against the prevailing tide of Abstract Expressionism, and was the result of careful thought and preparation.

When Anuszkiewicz appeared in 1960, he burst full blown into an art world unprepared for him. In fact, the term "Op art," which was afterward to be so frequently applied to his work, had not yet been coined. Many prominent art critics of the periodical press had focused their admiration for a decade or more on the Abstract Expressionist movement.

Anuszkiewicz's art is a reaction against Abstract Expressionism. It is planned rather than impulsive; it utilizes a uniform surface rather than manual traces; it is symmetrical rather than asymmetrical; it is calculated rather than accidental; it is impersonal rather than autobiographical; it uses repetition rather than uniqueness; it is intellectual rather than emotional; and it requires technical discipline rather than technical freedom. It is no wonder, then, that those critics who had espoused the art of the 1950s found this reversal difficult to accept.

Furthermore, the pictures Anuszkiewicz showed, with their juxtaposition of sharply contrasting colors in calculated geometric compositions, provoked an equivocal response in the eye of the observer, so that colors shifted and shimmered, forms reversed themselves, spatial interpretations were confounded.

The color experiments of Albers and others were already well known, and Victor Vasarely's theories of perception and color had been published in 1955. But in the United States no strong trend toward what came to be called "optical" (or "retinal" or "perceptual") art had been noted. Anuszkiewicz, himself, working with the ideas he had derived from his studies with Albers and the analytical concepts of his Yale thesis, was

14. Anuszkiewicz on rooftop with his paintings

15. Anuszkiewicz on rooftop with his paintings

only tangentially aware that other artists were exploring the territory he had chosen for himself.

The press notices given to that first New York exhibition (and others in succeeding years) were somewhat noncommittal or in some cases even hostile. The target of certain critics then (as it is occasionally even today) was Anuszkiewicz's "scientific" approach to painting[8] and the disorganizing effect upon the viewer. They said that his works "make havoc with normal vision"[9]; that "after lengthy looking at them, one cannot positively identify either shape or color"[10]; that they are "the precise conceptions of a scientific mind,"[11] embodying "recondite principles of color composition"[12]; that they stun the viewer and "dazzle, and perplex the eye"[13]; that they "titillate the eye with paintings whose colors and geometric patterns are so intense as to make one wince"[14]—"for sheer, active physical discomfort Anuszkiewicz's paintings rate high . . . create a jangling of the retina. The effect is like putting your finger in an electric socket"[15]; "the effect is dizzying, as though the viewer's eyes had gone out of focus."[16]

By 1964 the label "Op art" had come into broad currency, and Anuszkiewicz was referred to as an "Op painter" by most newspaper and magazine critics. In that year, in *The New York Times*, John Canaday and Grace Glueck both called him an "Op painter"; *Time* Magazine published an article titled "Op Art: Pictures That Attack the Eye,"[17] and *Life* Magazine, in an article called "Op Art: The Strange New Art That Tricks the Eye," named him "one of the new Wizards of Op."[18] From the start, his paintings in group exhibitions were singled out for mention and remarked upon for their compelling qualities, and he was characterized as the master of a movement.[19]

Most American critics of contemporary painting have avoided dealing with Op art, generally for reasons similar to those expressed by Hilton Kramer: "The victories [Anusz-

16. Working sketches

kiewicz's paintings] win over the spectator's visual attention are technically brilliant but expressively empty. Like many lesser votaries of optical painting, he forfeits the finer shades of feeling for surface effects. His virtuoso mastery of these effects remains impressive, but it is meager compensation for the emotional void that motivates it."[20] In much the same vein, Sidney Tillim said, "The bulk of optical art does not yet give pleasure"[21]; Barbara Rose said, "Op art has no expressive content. It is expressively neutral, having to do with sensation alone"[22]; and Lucy Lippard said that optical effects "held no lasting interest for most serious artists, who were more likely to be concerned with form, color, the poetic or formal expansion of painting than with perceptual effects alone."[23]

These comments, summing up a whole range of experiences, are characteristic of many critics dedicated to Abstract Expressionism, who expected an Expressionist content. That the paintings do have a strong effect is clear from the vehemence of some of the reactions quoted above. The fact that the pictures transmit their effects more immediately than Abstract Expressionism does not disqualify them as vehicles of expression. Anuszkiewicz's paintings produce sensations with no specific associations. In this sense they are related to music. Like music, his work is an art of ordered sensations. It is cool and impersonal and appeals to those who are searching for a shared human identity rather than an individually differentiated one. This probably accounts for Anuszkiewicz's immediate acceptance by the young, who found his work compatible with their own psychedelic interests, their acceptance of attacks upon the senses.

Let us test Anuszkiewicz in terms of Lucy Lippard's remarks as to the serious artist's concern with form, color, and the poetic or formal expansion of painting.

17. Anuszkiewicz in front of his paintings

Of course, these aspects of painting are precisely the concern of Anuszkiewicz. And when Sidney Tillim said that Op artists "failed to 'open' the grid and create a new kind of pictorial space without violating the picture plane with their illusionistic perceptual mirages,"[24] he ignored the contribution made by such artists as Anuszkiewicz, with his new forms of figure-ground relationship, his utilization of Gestalt principles of depth perception, and the structural tension of his picture surfaces.

As his formal structure Anuszkiewicz prefers symmetry, which has challenged him for many years. "When I first went to art school," he has said, "we were taught a Mondrianesque asymmetry; we were taught that one doesn't use clashing colors. But now I'm more interested in arithmetical or geometrical relationships—this new interest makes me work with a central image." By Mondrianesque asymmetry he meant that Mondrian, even in his most geometric overall compositions, used thick and thin lines and dark and light colors; this created asymmetry because of the weights of the lines or the colors.

Almost all of the earlier forms of painting composition dealt with problems of weight or gravitational pull—the visual weight of color or objects or size as a determinant of balance— just as traditional architectural construction dealt with gravity by piling up heavy load-bearing elements to hold buildings erect and intact against gravitational stress, strain, and thrust. Anuszkiewicz created a new type of pictorial construction—a structural design that might be likened to the modern architectural principle that R. Buckminster Fuller has called "tensegrity."

This term, which combines the concepts of "tension" and "integrity," grew out of Fuller's theories of "energetic geometry" and found concrete expression in such well-known inventions as his geodesic domes. In these buildings the force of gravity is counteracted by a system of light structural members held in continuous tension throughout a repeated pattern of triangular or quadrangular forms so that they lace "the entire structure into a single, finite, energetic embrace,"[25] as strong in one direction as in any other.

Without belaboring the analogy it is possible to see in Anuszkiewicz's two-dimensional compositions a similar "energetic embrace," an "energetic geometry" of his own, independent of the laws of gravity. There is no difference in pull between up or down, and each equal part holds the others in place. Thus his paintings have no top, bottom, or sides but are constructed like the tissues of the body in a form of antigravitation. This structure distinguishes his paintings in formal concept from other modes of abstraction such as Suprematism, Cubism, and Expressionism—all of which composed the surface in gravitational balance. In color also he achieves an interlocking balance similar to that of his composition. There is no foreground and no background in his most recent paintings. There is no figure and no ground, no dominance or subordination.

Contemporary artists who feel that new directions in art can be found by utilizing new mediums produce works that in the end utilize the same old forms of art. Earthworks, kinetic works, and light works not only use materials suggested in the Futurist Manifestos of 1909 and 1910, but also produce forms of asymmetrical balance developed through centuries of concern with gravitational forces. Process art, derived from existentialist concepts made popular by the Abstract Expressionists, involves procedures such as dumping earth or felt or metal on the floor or in a corner in the hope that the ordinary will be turned into art because of a new context. The idea is indebted philosophically to the Dadaists and formally to Arp and other artists who, before World War I, gave honor to the laws of chance. Anuszkiewicz, abandoning gravitational concepts in accord with new discoveries in architecture and space exploration, devised one of the first new compositional approaches in the twentieth century.

Symmetry is basic to this approach. Anuszkiewicz considers the function of art to be a move toward increasing order. He sees asymmetry as being on the side of nature and symmetry as the emblem of art. Geometry is the visual manifestation of symmetry and order. This is one of his motivations for relinquishing realistic painting, for most of the visible world outside—the world of life, growth, and movement—appears predominantly asymmetrical. Indeed, some scientists have theorized that the whole universe is moving toward an irreversible disorder. The second law of thermodynamics (as formulated in terms of entropy, or the measure of disorder at atomic or molecular levels) implies that the energy which keeps the natural system working is becoming progressively less available (that is, wasted) and that the universe, thus, is "running down" and resulting in chaos. In representational art asymmetry has been a characteristic of observed nature.

We think of that part of our visual experience which is not symmetrical and therefore related to nature as decoration. Françoise Henry[26], in discussing medieval Irish art, says that the asymmetrical spiral is associated with life in manuscript illumination and other forms of decoration, where it was used to depict vine tendrils, curving motions of animal forms, and other living images. Equivalence, rather than absolute symmetry, was so profoundly connected with the symbolism of life that when the spiral in those arts evolved toward complete symmetry about 1000 A.D., it lost significance as a figural image and became a precise pattern of artistic decoration.

Granted that those forms of art which deal with nature find expression in asymmetry, it is still true that both realistic and abstract artists—by selection of forms and colors, by schemes of composition and balance, by manipulation of lines and spatial illusionism and chiaroscuro—impose a degree of man-made order upon the representational or conceptual material they choose to present to the observer. Anuszkiewicz has said, "The best artists have always had a system. Rembrandt was systematic about light; the Impressionists were systematic about color." In his own striving for the order that he sees as the emblem of art, as distinguished from nature, he has found mathematical precision—geometry—to be one dependable formal structure.

The desire for order and symmetry is not a new one in human experience. In 1681 Thomas Burnet complained of the seemingly discordant arrangement of the stars: "What a beautiful Hemisphere they would have made, if they had been plac'd in rank and order, if they had been all dispos'd into regular figures, and the little ones set with due regard to the greater, Then all finisht and made up into one fair piece or great Composition, according to the rules of Art and Symmetry. What a surprizing beauty this would have been to the Inhabitants of the Earth? what a lovely Roof to our little World? This indeed might have given one some temptation to have thought that they had been all made for us."[27]

Another aspect of Anuszkiewicz's remove from the traditional concern with representing observed nature and his effort to give order through art is his hard-edge, razor-sharp interfacing of form and color. Gradations and continuities are shunned. His forms and colors collide with an abrupt impact. His

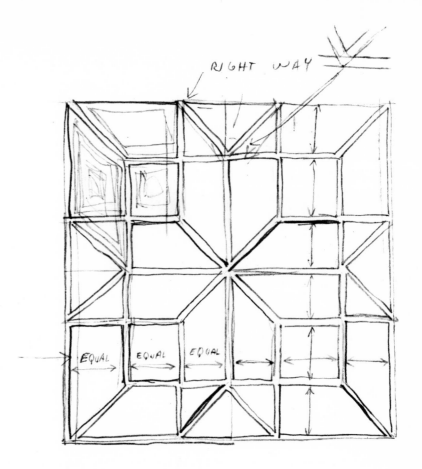

18. Working sketches

work, therefore, has a tactile and temporal quality: to experience it is to meet a world without any perspective or shading, like the tactile world of the blind, where encounters are sudden and all gradations of the visual world are gone.

Of course, paintings so highly controlled and ordered that they are singled out as "scientific" may induce a feeling of detachment that is often associated with scientific objectivity or impersonality. The spectator, under such conditions, may not feel involved. However, Anuszkiewicz does want to involve the viewer. "I try to manipulate [color] in schemes that give the viewer a particular feeling of excitement. If you want to call it emotion, that's fine."[28] In order to create this excitement he resorts to a physical stimulation of the optic nerve. This brings the painting to life and gives it an energy that is lacking in many geometric designs.

In a way his paintings bridge the seeming dichotomy between man-made order and pulsating life, for they state in visual form a mystery that hovers over both nature and science. Perhaps this is why he preferred for many of the paintings of his first adventures into geometric abstraction titles drawn from the field of alchemy, which was directed not only toward an understanding of the materials of the world but also toward a mystical resolution of life.

Anuszkiewicz has worked consistently on his concept of transparency. As he says, "One sees the color as substantial at one point and insubstantial at another point; each band seems successively more opaque; the bands make it seem transparent." Transparency is related to the x-ray photograph; one shape is placed against another so that you see things through each other, simultaneously and without dominance. In this interpenetration and transparency everything is locked together; no form overshadows any other. This is consistent with the tensegrity of the surface. For most artists, an object is defined in terms of the unique space it fills, as well as its relation to objects occupying other spaces.

Anuszkiewicz depicts space and forms occupying space as an interpenetration of equal objects in a web without seams. Here again, in this interpenetration and interaction, the analogy of his work with science seems apposite. It is almost as if he creates an electric field, within which positively and negatively charged bodies exert their opposed attractions or repulsions across space, growing stronger in close proximity and more tenuous at greater distance. At the same time the properties of heat and cold in his colors seem to flow and interact like thermodynamic transfers of energy. The energy of color is released as two lines of different colors approach one another in measured relationships, and it is this *color energy* that Anuszkiewicz studies. It is similar to what Albers called "Interaction of Color" and is a basic concept in Anuszkiewicz's painting.

He works with colors much as a poet works with words. The poet juxtaposes or arranges words so that their characteristics of sound and meaning reflect upon one another, interchanging forces that transform each one in relation to the others. Just so, Anuszkiewicz's colors, when brought together or set in calculated separation, unlock their inherent powers, let off their color discharges and their luminescence to interact in new ways. This is the poetry of his paintings.

The impetus given by European artists such as Victor Vasarely and the Groupe de Recherche d'art Visuel (founded in 1960) helped to establish Op as a movement. Although it was slow to be accepted by the critics, no movement of the last twenty-five years has made so swift an impact upon the public, nor, for better or worse, has been so instantly translatable into

19. Fur coat. 1963. Painted on calfskin for Jacques Kaplan, New York. Photograph in *Vogue*, as worn by Beatrice Lillie

the mass media in innumerable commercial applications of its principles. Its inherent directness may explain the immediate appeal of Op art.

By 1963, Richard Anuszkiewicz had designed gift wrappings, fur coats (plate 19), stockings, rugs (plate 127), banners, fabrics, and other items such as silver animals for Tiffany. This kind of adaptation from his paintings introduced, between his own inspiration and personal execution, the hands of craftsmen in several other fields. At the time there was a tendency to undervalue the work of artists whose designs reached the marketplace in the form of such merchandise, though cultural snobbery is somewhat baffling in the context of the 1960s, when many of the elite forms of art were heavily exploited. For a pupil of Albers, such as Anuszkiewicz, the field of applied art is perfectly consistent with Bauhaus attitudes. The Bauhaus was a school of design. There was no differentiation between artist and artisan. Packaging, furniture, advertising, and linoleum design were paralleled by the more traditional instruction in painting, sculpture, and architecture—a utopian application of a system to all phases of life. Richard Anuszkiewicz does not evaluate one form of art against another. His view of the world is essentially unhierarchical, enabling him to approach all design problems with enthusiasm.

In 1965 the Museum of Modern Art in New York mounted an exhibition called "The Responsive Eye," bringing together a major coverage of painters who were working with anomalies of visual perception. The disparities among them were perhaps almost as great as the affinities. In the case of Anuszkiewicz, who was prominently represented there, some of these similarities and differences may be illuminated by the following discussions of his development as an artist, his working methods, and his present position in relation to the Op art milieu.

20. Anuszkiewicz painting fur coat

21. *Plus Reversed*. 1960. Oil on canvas,
    74 1/2 × 58". University of Texas, Austin
    (The Michener Collection)

Anuszkiewicz's paintings can be divided into three periods: in his early works he was concerned with color mix and figure-ground relationships; he then began a period of experimentation with black-and-white modules to solve problems of shape illusion on two- and three-dimensional surfaces; in the resulting current period of his work he deals with color mix by the use of lines and works with problems of transparency and surface tensegrity.

The directions indicated by his *Mask* of 1955 and by his Yale thesis on line were not continued immediately. He became more interested in optical color mix and began to study different means of effecting it, working with the problems of color change and of adjacent color influence.

If a color is made by physically mixing two pigments, full intensity is sacrificed; the color becomes grayer. For example, red and yellow mixed produce orange, but it is a grayed orange, different from pure cadmium orange. The intensity and integrity of the colors can be maintained if they are mixed not on the palette but by the eye of the viewer, as in Pointillism.

At first Anuszkiewicz worked with meandering or undulating forms, but then his forms became more fixed. An early example of this is his use of the almost random plus signs of *Plus Reversed* (1960, plate 21). At this time, he painted in oil pigments brushed on by hand, so that there is an unevenness in the shapes of *Plus Reversed*. There is also a quality of randomness in the casual scattering of the forms at the edges as they tilt in one direction or another, becoming more consistently placed at the center. It is at this point that red figures on a green ground change to green figures on a red ground; the relative nature of red as a hot color and green as a cool color is shown by their fluctuating advance and retreat from the spectator.

While Anuszkiewicz is very much interested in the Pointillist concept of color interaction, he believes that a theory of color is not workable. For example, he said, "You can make anything advance or recede. If you surround a dark brown or blue with yellow, other factors make it recede or advance. What's next to it is what's important. Signac used colors in a realistic way—the colors of his foregrounds are brighter, and as they go into the distance they become paler—realism controlled his color. And his real limitation was his insistence on a distinct foreground and background."

Plus Reversed is a striking example of figure-ground relationships in Gestalt perception. His main concern here is not order but color mix.

In a search for greater control of the medium—as in *Triangular Prism* (1962, plate 22)—Anuszkiewicz began to use plastic templates, mechanical cutouts that allow the forms to remain undeviatingly regular. He demanded more and more control of the actual execution and of the graduation of color in the mix. This could not be done freehand with the degree of subtlety and precision that he sought. In this painting dots in blue and green move horizontally and vertically on a red ground. The format is related to the square within the square previously dealt with in terms of pure and unambiguous shapes. But here there is strong ambiguity: toward the center the blue dots grow smaller, and the green dots grow larger. As they pass each other, they neutralize each other. The plan is one of arithmetical progression. Anuszkiewicz had often used geometrical progression (i.e., a doubling or multiplying of shapes) as the plan of his compositions, but arithmetical progression is slower, allowing for denser effects. He eventually came to use arithmetical progression in his line paintings in order to control color mix.

Mathematics is used by Anuszkiewicz as a beginning, just as a nude or a still life might be used by another artist. Mathematics provides his idea, his plan; his paintings make the plan visible. The effect produced by using either arithmetical or geometrical progression is one of expanding or contracting densities, determined by the intervals. Intervals are basic to art forms from dance and music to architecture and sculpture.

He briefly experimented with the use of dots freely brushed on by hand, each dot evenly juxtaposed. *All Things Do Live in the Three* (1963, plate 23) has an illusion of transparency. In the interpenetration of colors three diamond forms appear. This device maintains the surface while giving the illusion of an interpenetration of that surface. It is illusionistic painting primarily concerned with figure-ground relationships.

Anuszkiewicz's preference for line developed from an interest in color, and the colored line was the solution. He realized that the most subtle color mix could be achieved by the manipulation of colored lines—either a similarly colored group of lines on a changing ground or a line that might change color several times over a uniformly colored ground. To achieve controlled linear effects, he decided to use architects' charting tapes, as explained on page 62.

Whereas *Plus Reversed* and *Triangular Prism* are opposites in one sense, the first producing sudden figure-ground change and the second, gradual figure-ground change and color mixing, they are alike in preserving the tensegrity of the surface; in neither is there a clear-cut distinction between foreground and background. Thus they are not related to older

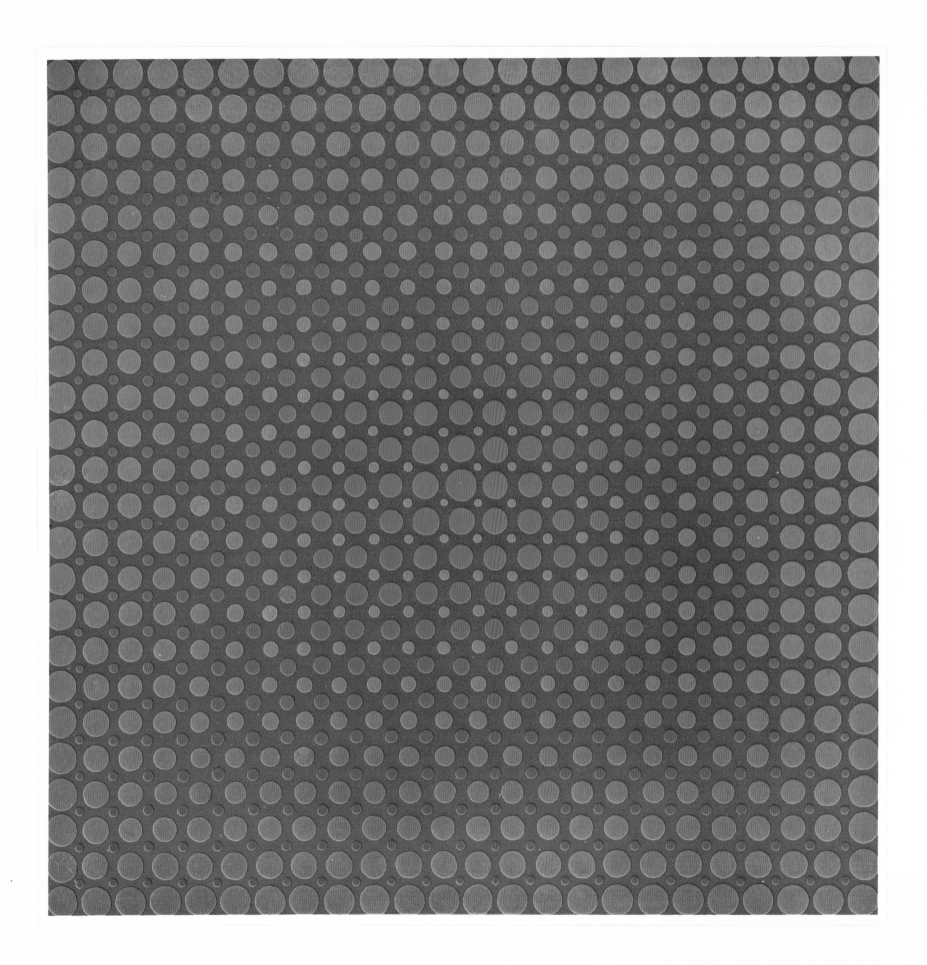

23. *All Things Do Live in the Three*. 1963. Acrylic on Masonite, 21 7/8 × 35 7/8″. Collection Mrs. Robert M. Benjamin, New York

22. *Triangular Prism*. 1962. Acrylic on Masonite, 23 7/8 × 23 7/8″.
Collection Mrs. Robert M. Benjamin, New York

forms of perspective painting which produce spatial illusion at the expense of the integrity of the surface. Space or spatial illusion of some sort—either clear or ambiguously fluctuating—is always to be found in the juxtaposition of any two colors, but this is not the point of either of these paintings. Line functions as a means of color mix, not of spatial illusion.

Anuszkiewicz has always had a preference for the square canvas, even in his juvenile paintings before his exposure to Albers. In time he came up against the obstacle that the eye tends to perceive a mathematically exact square as wider than it is high. Increasing the height will make a blank canvas appear square, but when it is subdivided geometrically, the inequality of the elements will be obvious. If the artist is a perfectionist, these factors must be considered or even countered in some way. Beginning with this observation, that the eye is deceived about shape, Anuszkiewicz did a series of experiments in which the image on the canvas would rectify the perceptual distortion in some cases and exaggerate it in others.

Thus he found that geometry was opposed to Gestalt, or simplest and most natural illusion. That is why he decided to work with Gestalt instead of geometry alone, and how he came to illusionism, because Gestalt is illusion. This led to a most fertile period in his career, during which he used a modular system of black-and-white painting in two and three dimensions, with line as force rather than as color.

Concerned as Anuszkiewicz was with edges and borders in his paintings, it is natural to ask why he never experimented with the shaped canvas. Since the edge of the canvas is the context within which the image is created, he preferred to emphasize the border, frequently with a color of its own. When a canvas is shaped in some special way, it becomes an element in a larger composition—the wall: the four boundaries of the wall

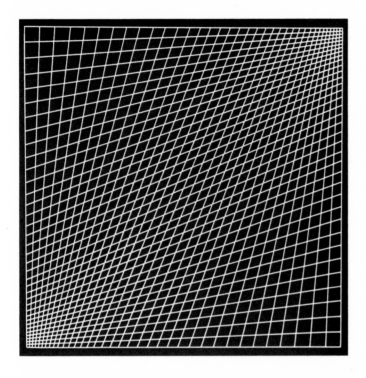

24. *Unit.* 1966. Acrylic on Masonite,
16 × 16″. Collection Karl Lunde, New York

become the canvas edges. Anuszkiewicz tried to confine the experience within the margins of the canvas rather than to create an environment in which the painting is a fragment. He realized the need to establish the borders of the painting so that people will not seek them in the borders of the room.

He painted a series of canvases in black and white during this period, all deriving from a single work, *Unit* (1966, plate 24). This single square unit forms a grid pattern that expands in two opposite corners and contracts in the other two opposite corners, creating an illusionistic distortion of a flat surface. If the unit is used as a module, four duplicates when placed together produce either a contracting or an expanding center, depending upon juxtaposition (either *Concave 1* [1966, plate 27] or *Convex 2* [1966, plate 28]. Anuszkiewicz thereby has created the illusion of a shaped canvas.

By combining six units in a work called *Convex and Concave* (1966, plate 25), he created a double center—an interesting development for a painter who had worked so long with a central image. There is in this work the appearance of the overlapping of the two separate paintings *Concave 1* and *Convex 2*.

Ideas proliferated quickly after that. Having explored combinations of two, four, and six, he wanted to work with three. Since there is no way to combine three on a flat surface with a unified edge, he turned to the cube (three sides of which can be seen at one time). He then worked with a half-cube seen from the inside by placing three units in a corner of the room (1967, plate 26), one lying flat on the floor, and one placed vertically on the wall at each side of the corner.

Anuszkiewicz intended exhibiting these black paintings with their white grids against a black wall: he wanted the white grids to be figure. The cubes and corner pieces came out of the

47

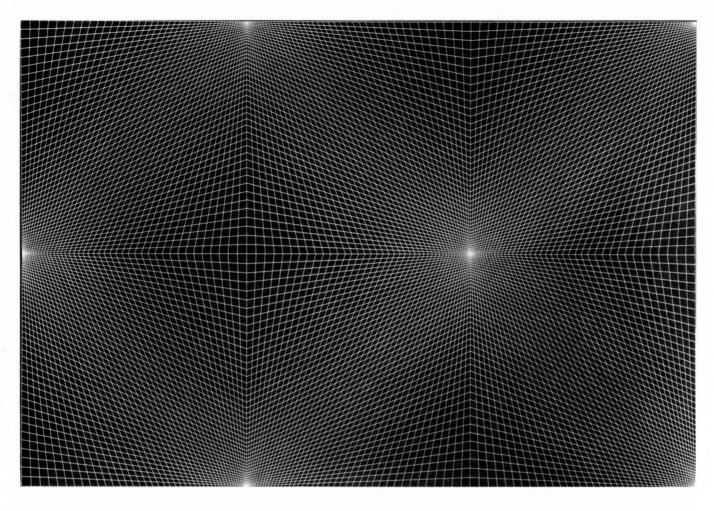

25. *Convex and Concave.* 1966.
    Acrylic on canvas, 72 × 108″.
    Private collection

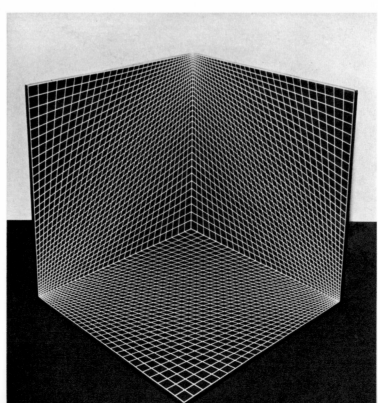

26. *Convex & Concave, III: Dimensional.*
1967. Enamel on plywood, three 32″ squares.
Collection the artist

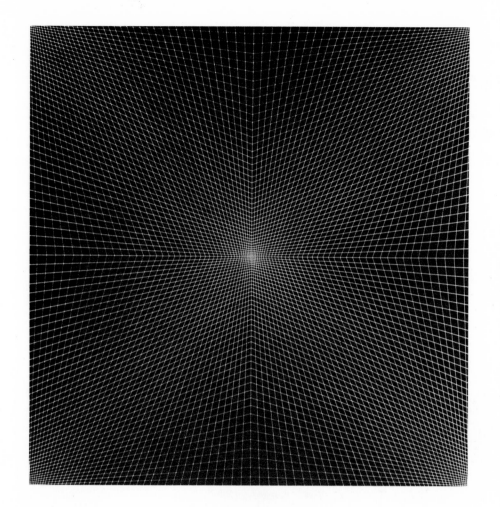

27. *Concave 1*. 1966. Acrylic on canvas, each panel 7 1/2 × 7 1/2'. The Ratner Family Collection, Fort Lee, N.J.

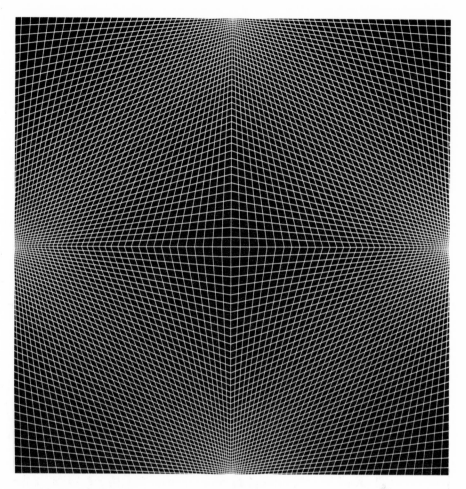

28. *Convex 2*. 1966. Acrylic on canvas, each panel 7 1/2 × 7 1/2'. The Ratner Family Collection, Fort Lee, N.J.

study of the module. Just as the *Convex, Concave* paintings were explorations of Gestalt principles, so were the three-dimensional pieces. Gestalt psychologists imply that the whole is more than the sum of the parts. *Convex and Concave* (1966) is made up of six modules, the same as those which form the six faces of the cube. Two separate works, one flat and one three-dimensional, were made up of exactly the same parts but added up to completely different wholes.

Since Anuszkiewicz did not consider the cubes to be sculpture in any conventional sense, he rejected the idea of placing them on pedestals; at the same time he realized that placing the cube on a mirror would double the image. He began to think then of the total image as the sum of the image plus its reflection, presenting the eye with the illusion of a quantity twice its actuality. *Convex & Concave, 1: Dimensional* (1967, plate 30) was the result.[29]

His color cubes were done subsequently and compose a series of their own. The one called *Spiral* (1967, plate 29) has green and blue lines on a red surface and is based upon its own module. The lines travel diagonally across each surface, but when put on a mirror they seem to continue all around the cube. Since the color values are close to each other and each side of a cube is lighted differently, the volume becomes more pronounced than the surface; therefore Anuszkiewicz abandoned this idea. In the black-and-white cubes, the graphic contrast is so strong that the grid pattern dominates the volume.

A square, if divided diagonally, will result in two triangles, or four if divided twice. On point, the square becomes a diamond. For Anuszkiewicz, working with the problem of the square on point was an extension of his many paintings from the first half of the 1960s which had a square on point within the format of a square. *Longitudinal—Latitudinal* (1966, plate 31) consists of two large square panels, placed side by side, touching at one point. The visual stress in the left diamond is vertical, in the right one, horizontal. They are two of the original modular units. Perfect diamonds in reality, they appear distorted, although each unit is square. Tilting them in this way creates a different shape (a diamond) from the previous one (a square), and they have two different kinds of perceptual distortion. When they are so juxtaposed, point to point, a maximum distortion results because of the opposing forces of the two panels (the vertical and horizontal distortion of plane surfaces).

29. *Spiral.* 1967. Enamel on plywood, on mirrored base, 24″ cube. Collection the artist

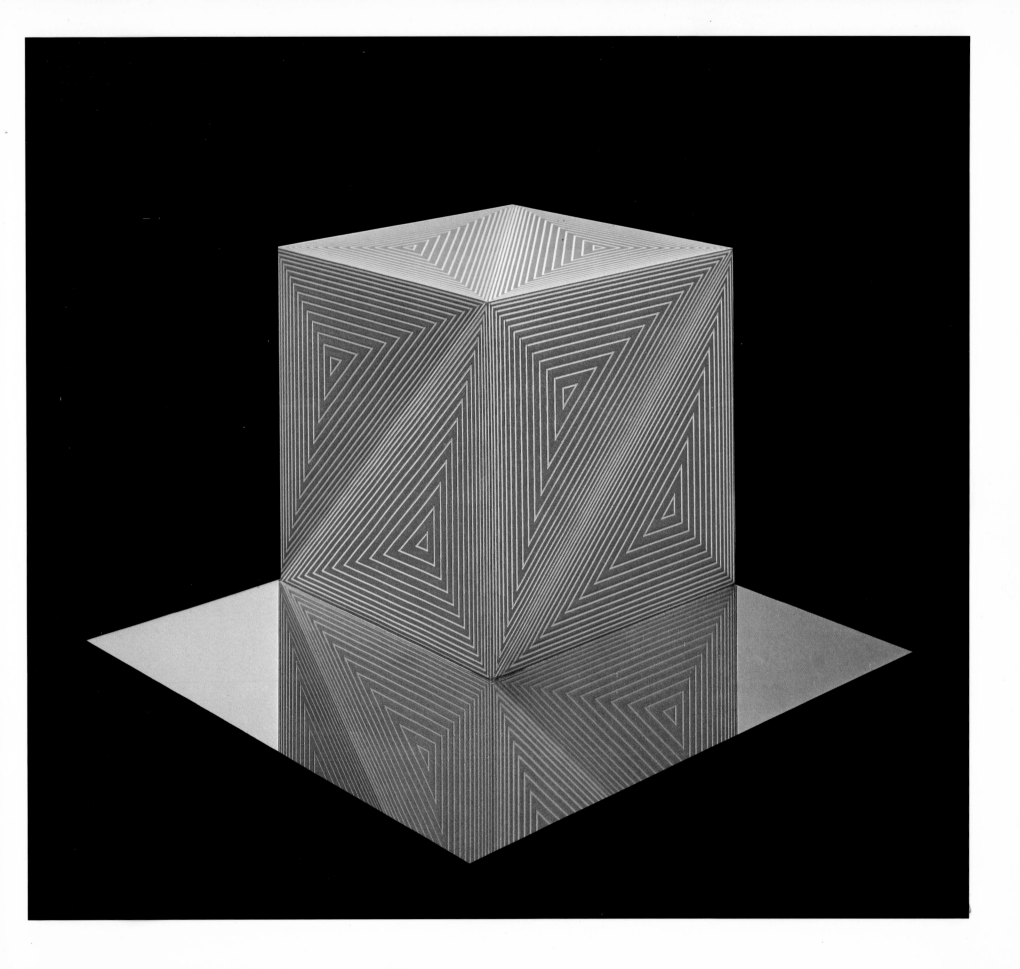

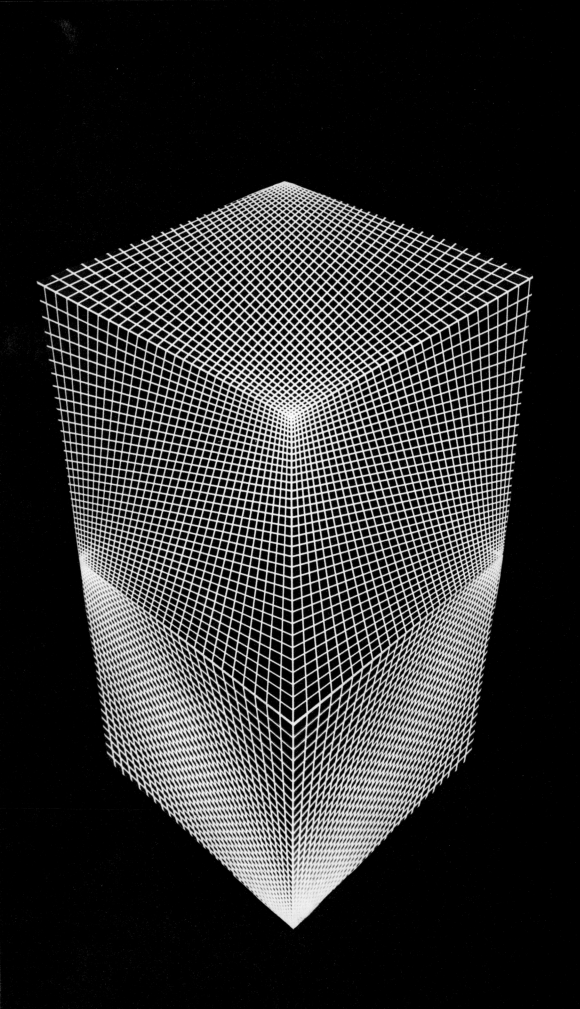

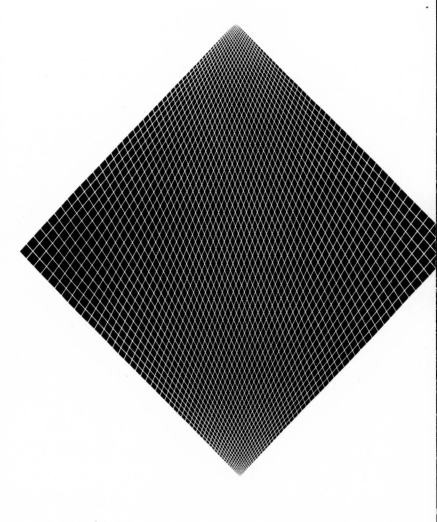

30. *Convex & Concave, I: Dimensional.* 1967. Enamel
on plywood, on mirrored base, 32″ cube.
The Albright-Knox Art Gallery, Buffalo, N.Y.
(gift of Seymour H. Knox)

By putting the vertical unit next to the horizontal unit, this distinction is made clear.

We are dealing with illusionistic painting, then: something is made to seem other than it is. However, a differentiation should be made between spatial illusions, which are used to create depth in a painting, and the illusion of shape. Anuszkiewicz's paintings have, with rare exceptions, not been spatially illusionistic, because they maintain the integrity of the surface; there is no pull into space. They have instead created an illusionistic distortion of the canvas shape.

For Anuszkiewicz line is normally color, a means of creating the color mixes that concern him. But in his black-and-white paintings line serves a different function. It is force, a distorting force. It is energy, just as color is energy of a different kind. His entire procedure of work, with its apparent preoccupation with lines, has not been for the sake of the lines themselves (any more than his technique has been one of precision for precision's sake) but rather for the various densities, color changes, and distortions that could possibly result.

Sometimes another distortion, the illusion of transparency, has concerned him. *Prisma* (1968, plate 32), a six-part modular unit, is an example; in it the illusion of six transparent diamonds is created by placing six squares together. Since the pigment is not transparent, this painting is illusionistic also.

Following his experiments in black and white, Anuszkiewicz returned to a study of visual color mixing, using fine lines at varying intervals.

In *Moonbow* (1968, plate 33) he varied the ground vertically from orange at the left to red at the right and divided the canvas into four spaces from left to right, moving from pale blue, to green-blue, to green, to yellow-green. In each square the lines become more concentrated at the edges, creating a glow there, and the red and orange centers change as the

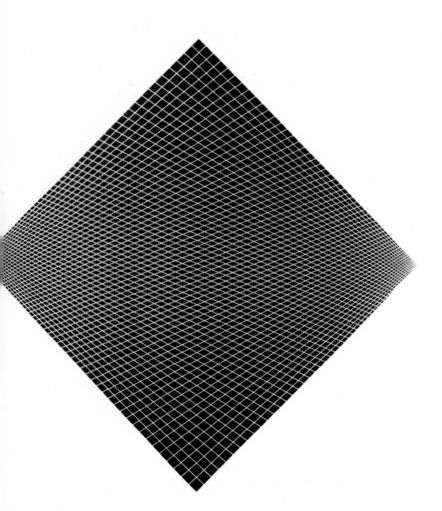

31. *Longitudinal—Latitudinal.* 1966.
   Acrylic on canvas, each panel 60 × 60".
   Collection the artist

32. *Prisma.* 1968. Acrylic on canvas, 72 × 108″. Collection Katherine C. White, Los Angeles

33. *Moonbow*. 1968. Acrylic on canvas, 48 × 48″. Collection Mr. and Mrs. M. Rikles, New York

spaces between the lines increase toward the center. This painting is an entity which becomes a module in later paintings, just as *Unit* (1966) had become a module in his black-and-white studies.

Grand Spectra (1968, plate 37) consists of four paintings, each progressing from red in one corner to yellow in the opposite corner, and each overlaid with blue or green lines. Placed together, the four paintings create a symmetry, but this can be varied by rearranging them to put red in the center of the whole, or in the center of the edge, or in the corner. There is an effect of transparency within each square, but a much more complex transparency is achieved in the total composition where various geometric patterns can be read, such as squares within squares, crosses within squares, and diamonds within squares.

The ability of the exhibitor to vary the composition leads naturally to later variables such as the *Coaster Tray* (plate 36) produced by *Art in America* (1970), *Orange Delight* (1969, plate 34), and the multiple *Centum* (1970, plate 35), which is discussed at greater length on page 65.

Richard Anuszkiewicz's concept of unity is not one of dominance and subordinance. Rather, it is additive: a whole of equal parts put together. His composition might be called "democratic"—the aggregate of equal parts to form a new unit—as opposed to a Baroque composition subjected to a hierarchy of order. In his modular three-dimensional works he tries to show that a total is neither the sum of the parts nor a hierarchy.

We have seen that his compositions of the sixties were self-contained and centralized, and that his colors were abrupt and ambiguous, being equally figure and ground.

His modular paintings of the late sixties, additive in con-

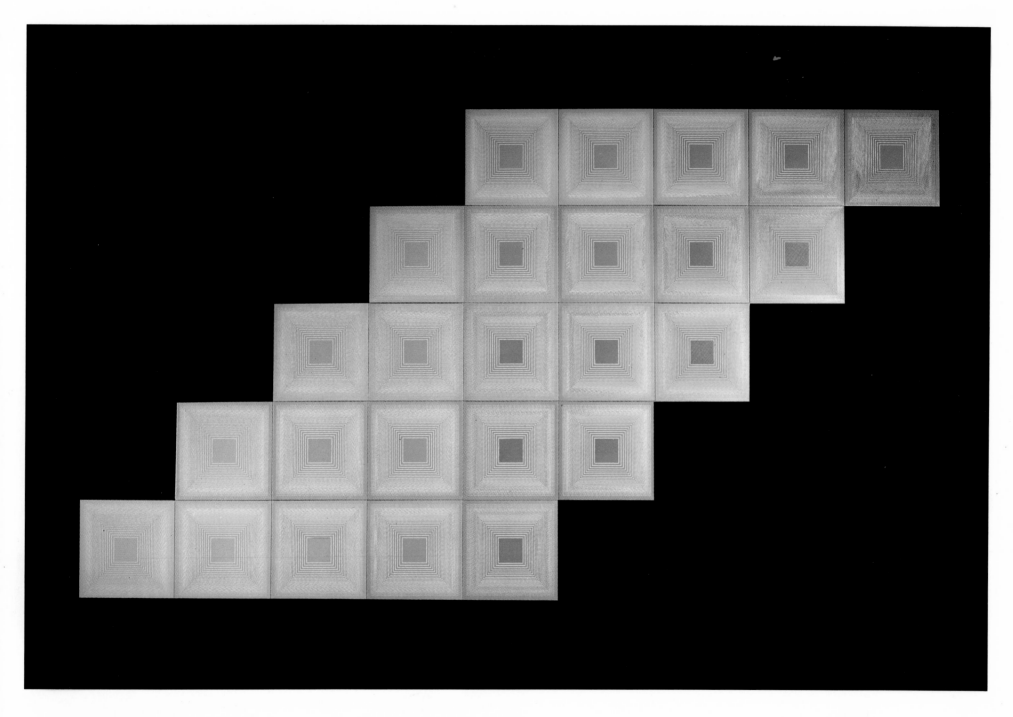

34. *Orange Delight.* 1969. Acrylic on canvas, 10 × 18′; twenty-five panels each 24 × 24″. The Whitney Museum of American Art, New York

37. *Grand Spectra*. 1968. Acrylic on canvas, 10 × 10′. The Art Commission for the South Mall Project, Albany State Capitol

35. *Centum*. 1970. Porcelain enamel on steel, four groups of twenty-five tiles (100 in all), variable within the four groups, 82 × 82″ overall. Multiple for Abrams Original Editions, New York

36. Coaster tray. 1970. Porcelain enamel on steel, nine pieces, each 4 1/2 × 4 1/2″. Multiple produced by *Art in America*

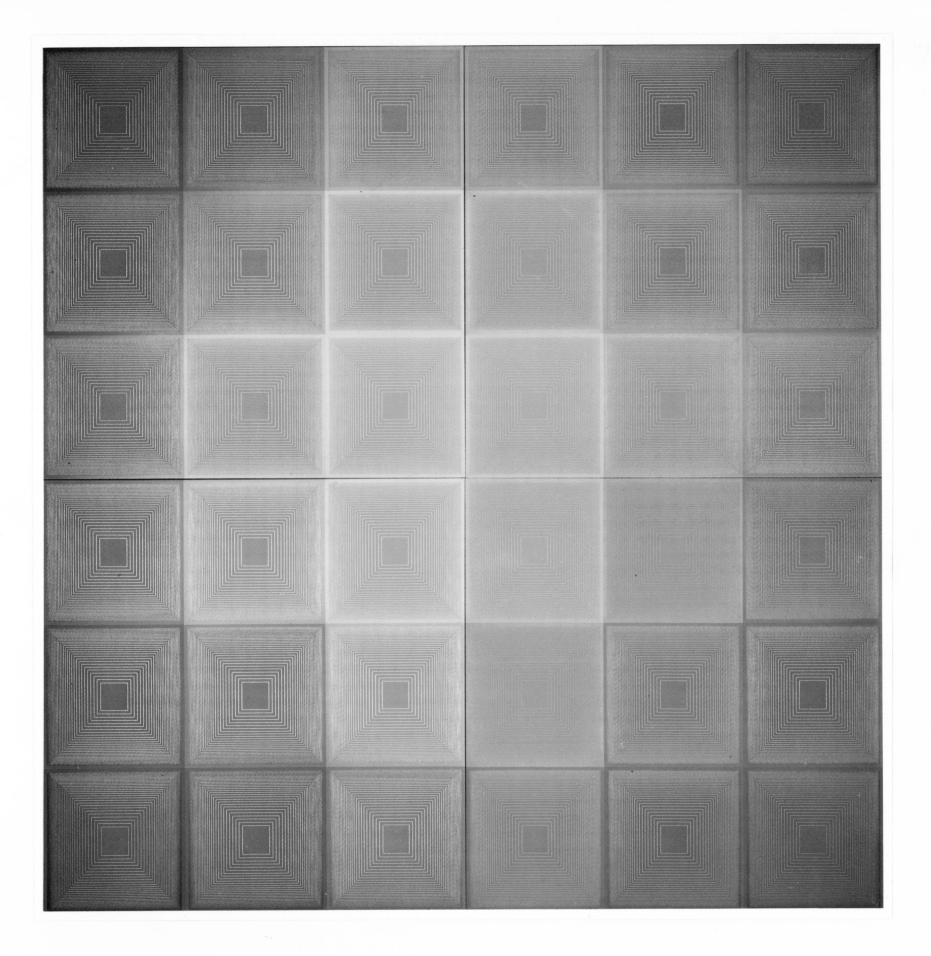

cept, implied that by repetition they could be extended beyond their present existence.

This gradual movement into the spectator's space has culminated in his paintings of the mid-seventies. The composition has become peripheral and carries the suggestion that a world of greater density and color, less neutral and more varied, lies beyond the picture surface. It is as if the colors have repelled each other, so that some take refuge at the edge, while others hold their ground but are derived from the dominant color.

The center of the painting is now flat and noncommittal, with bands that dance across it, or small, regularly spaced lines on the edges that act as rulers, speedometers, or thermometers measuring infinite distances, speeds, and temperatures. The colors of the edges always progress in a perceivable but mysterious order, a spectrum of some new, unexplored prismatic range. In all of this there are rules and order, yet an observation of the system indicates that nothing remains constant within this order.

There are some things we can understand only by measurement, since they are either invisible or infinite. Energy is one of these things, as are speed, temperature, and space. Our knowledge of these aspects of the world is theoretical, and the only concrete evidence we have of their existence is measurement that we read by instruments. Therefore, to deal with the subject of measurement is to deal with one of the fundamentals of understanding.

This point of view is a natural development of Richard Anuszkiewicz's method of working: planning the painting in a mathematical, theoretical way, while in another room the actual painting is brought into existence by an assistant who follows his instructions, who translates his measurements and color notes into paintings on canvas.

38. Anuszkiewicz at work

Although Anuszkiewicz's paintings have the appearance of exacting precision, in fact they are the product of trial and error. He propounds no theory in them; rather, they reveal a searching interest in the phenomenon of color. He conceives of himself as a problem solver who sets up the problem he wishes to resolve. There is no scientific solution beyond the one that pleases Anuszkiewicz aesthetically, and each solution leads to the next problem.

He does not give great importance to his technique, because he sees it as mechanical. "Planning is the creative part;

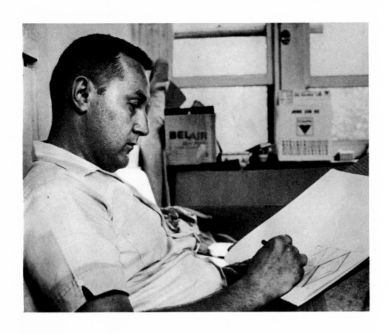

39. Anuszkiewicz planning his work

decision making is the creative part. It's possible to have assistants as long as you have control, and it's no different from an architect planning a building. What I do is closer to that, obviously, than to something like Abstract Expressionism, where ideas develop with the brushstroke itself. Here the plan is important, with some allowances for changes in the idea at certain stages. One makes decisions beforehand, carries them through, and adjustments are made at the time of working.''

No technique, no theory can, in itself, produce masterworks. If it could, every Pointillist would have produced a painting on the level of Georges Seurat's *La Grande Jatte*. As Anuszkiewicz sees it, technique should always serve the image that the artist wishes to present: it is a means, not an end. He believes that personal experimentation will lead the artist to the proper technique for his particular image, but that the application of an approach is of no value unless there is an idea behind it.

Because his technique has puzzled some observers, it should be described briefly here, although by this time it is certainly known to art students.

For smaller paintings, Anuszkiewicz uses Masonite panels, but the problems of warping on that surface are such that for his larger works he substitutes canvas to avoid irregular or ragged pulling of the architectural charting tapes that he has adopted to ensure the exactness of his lines and color edges. These tapes, which he began to use not long after his experiments with colored dots in 1963 (e.g., plate 23), are narrow gummed plastic strips, available in widths varying from 1/16 to 1/4 inch. They can be applied, like masking tape, to a prepared surface. In ordinary use they indicate lines on charts or graphs and can be easily removed or replaced in different

40. Anuszkiewicz and assistant,
Ann Davis, at work

configurations. Also, to obtain the even surface that he prefers,
he uses cotton rather than linen canvas.

On the canvas he first applies three coats of polymer
(acrylic) gesso, sanding each coat. His colors must be mixed in
advance, because acrylic paint looks very different when dry. The
mixing is done under a uniform warm light in a room away from
his large studio, and swatches are made to test the effect of the
color after drying. The swatches must also be varnished, because varnish will be applied in a later phase, and it too changes
the color intensity. Anuszkiewicz mixes the full quantity of paint
necessary for the completion of any one painting, because later
approximations of hue, value, or saturation will not work. Uni-

41. Color scales prepared by Anuszkiewicz

formity is of the essence in solving each color problem he sets himself.

Then the color selected to appear as lines in the painting is brushed over the surface with soft sable brushes. Five coats of water-thinned acrylic paint are needed to build up the desired opacity and intensity. When the color is completely dry, the artist coats the painting with a thinned varnish (gloss medium) to prevent any possibility of bleeding through in successive color applications. A sponge is used to varnish large areas quickly without brushstrokes.

At this point the very narrow charting tapes are applied in measured patterns on the surface of the painting, a new color is applied over this, and the tapes are removed to reveal the underpaint. This process is repeated as often as required. Anuszkiewicz does not paint lines; he paints the entire surface. The color underneath, which is uncovered when the tapes are lifted, is what appears as lines.

Despite all his careful preliminary testing, Anuszkiewicz overpaints frequently until the desired color mix is achieved.

The precisely controlled working methods of his paintings obviously lend themselves to printmaking techniques, and Anuszkiewicz has been prolific in the print field. Closest of all the print media to his chosen painting techniques is the silkscreen; he finds that medium congenial because it affords both opacity of color and the clean abutment of color areas that his images require. His first print was made in 1963. Since then he has produced a number of portfolios and suites for publishers in Europe and in the United States. Among these are a suite of six serigraphs for Galerie der Spiegel, Cologne, in 1965, and a portfolio of ten serigraphs called *Inward Eye* (1970), published by Aquarius Press, New York.

He has also worked in lithography, though at first it presented him with greater technical difficulties in that the register of adjacent colors and the transparency of some inks may result in overlapping edges which show up as unwanted lines. For that reason his earliest lithographs were done in black and white. His first color lithograph, *Yellow Reversed,* 1970 (printed by offset as an insert in *Art in America*), was a successful solution of his technical problems. He chose to execute it in one color, pure cadmium yellow, using the white of the paper as contrast. "The idea of a side-by-side double image, where the figure-and-ground relationship has been reversed, was inspired by the folded sheet (or gatefold) of this print insert."[30]

Apart from prints on paper (which include some very large screen prints to serve as posters for exhibitions at the Museum of Modern Art, in New York; the Corcoran Gallery Biennial of 1965, in Washington, D.C.; and the second Buffalo Festival of the Fine Arts Today, 1968), Anuszkiewicz has designed multiples for other surfaces. He used porcelain enamel tiles for the multiple called *Centum* (1970, plate 35). This work consisted of one hundred tiles assembled in four square sections of twenty-five tiles each, in red transmuting to orange and yellow across a greenish grid provided by the tile edges. Because of the durability of the material, the work could be installed out of doors. Also, the color composition could be varied by rearranging the sections, though the artist had established a preferred order in the original sequence.

This kind of multiple, like the commercial products mentioned earlier, requires the skills of craftsmen trained to execute the designs envisioned by the artist.

Anuszkiewicz's interest in working with assistants, which

he compares with the architect's use of carpenters and masons, made him eager to work on, and his conceptions suitable to, the creation of exterior murals. Two commissions in this field were carried out in 1972—one on an office building near Journal Square in Jersey City, not far from his home, and the other on the side of a Y.W.C.A. building in New York City (plate 42). His art is unusually suited for this large-scale form because its emphasis on rectangularity acts as an extension of the architecture and its surroundings, adding the element of color.

About the New York wall he said: "In sunlight the warm colors brighten and the cool colors darken. At dusk the reverse happens."[31] A New York critic, not easily won over to any outdoor murals at all, conceded that the work "is a fine job and an addition to the cityscape" because it "does not use the wall simply as a gigantic canvas arbitrarily decorated but adjusts itself respectfully to the location it occupies, as every mural indoors or outdoors should do."[32]

Despite his youthful experience as a house painter, Anuszkiewicz does not attempt to apply the colors personally to these city walls. He prepares the cartoon for the murals and he mixes the paints himself for color accuracy, but the direct application is turned over to professional sign or billboard painters up on their scaffolds working under his direction.

For the artist himself, projects of this kind provide a welcome stimulus, different from the problems of studio paintings. Working with another scale, another surface, he finds this new departure restorative and contributive of fresh approaches. At present he looks forward to another similar challenge—a "plaza painting" to give focus to a development of the New York waterfront.

Some indication of his own aims and interests as an artist and his working hypotheses may be gleaned from Anuszkie-

wicz's responses to works of other periods and styles. It is not surprising that the architectural qualities of certain painters—Uccello, Piero della Francesca, and Vermeer, among others—would appeal to Anuszkiewicz, but the wide range of his interests is revealed by his affinity for artists from many periods and cultures. This is one more aspect of his unhierarchical view of the world.

For example, of Rubens's *Rape of the Daughters of Leucippus* (plate 43), he says: "It's too fleshy. I prefer Uccello, with his strong diagonals. Or Vermeer or Piero della Francesca—who *construct,* with strongly placed objects. Here it is just one big mass, one thing blends into another. I like more clearly defined things. Here, there's nothing for contemplation: all the action is in the painting, there's nothing for you to do—it's all done for you. It's too obvious—very unintellectual. It's an illustration. So many painters who deal with Biblical themes or mythology are really illustrators in the sense that they lose their concern for the formal problems in their concern for storytelling. For me the way it's done is more important. Rubens's simplest paintings interest me more. Take for example *La Petite Pelisse* (*The Fur Cloak*), (plate 44). It has simplicity, and I'm always attracted to simplicity. What is beautiful here is the interesting light and dark of the figure, the almost black background, the way the body is cut right in half—this is a very dramatic factor. And it's not too fleshy—there's a lot more for the imagination. The whole problem in painting is: what is just the right amount? The usual mistake that painters make is to do too much or not enough—balance is what you work for."

Concerning Jan van Eyck's *Annunciation* in Washington (plate 45), he says: "I immediately see it as a part of something. There is a cut-off quality about it—it must be the left-

42. Exterior mural, Y.W.C.A. Building, New York. 1972. c. 100 × 70'.

43. Peter Paul Rubens. *The Rape of the Daughters of Leucippus.*
    c. 1615–17. Oil on canvas, 87 1/2 × 82 1/4". Alte Pinakothek, Munich

hand part of a larger altarpiece, a triptych. The lack of symmetry, moving from the left and then cut off abruptly tells you that. His use of multiples is interesting here; I like his play with multiple areas. As to the individual meaning of the symbols—that's too subjective. I really look at it as an abstraction; I enjoy the play of the shapes. Now this is more complex than the Rubens *Leucippus.* The imagination is brought into play;

44. Peter Paul Rubens. *La Petite Pelisse (The Fur
    Cloak).* c. 1638. Oil on wood, 69 1/4 × 32 5/8".
    Kunsthistorisches Museum, Vienna

45. Jan van Eyck. *The Annunciation.* c. 1428.
Oil on wood transferred to canvas, 69 1/4 × 14 1/2".
National Gallery of Art, Washington, D.C.
(Mellon Collection)

you participate more. A fascinating use of horizontals and verticals opposed to diagonals."

Mondrian's *Composition with Red, Yellow, and Blue* (1930, plate 46) elicits the following response from Anuszkiewicz: "There is a lot for the eye to play with here, the edge against the red and the other colors as well as against the white, and the white areas themselves. The red and yellow are light. They would not be light if there were no black; these light colors would be darker colors. He also varies the thickness and thinness of the black lines. And there is a foreground-background play, both two- and three-dimensional: are the shapes against a white background, is the white in front of the colors, or on the same plane? Is it a grid or not? Not all the time."

A particular favorite of Anuszkiewicz's is Toshusai Sharaku, whose concern with space and placement seems related to his own. Concerning Sharaku's woodcut *Segawa Tomisaburo in Female Character* (plate 47), he says: "The concern here is with interval and placement; this kind of concern with detail is an ingrained part of the Japanese culture. Isolated things—one flower, for example. None of the vulgarity of Expressionism. Here there is a Mondrianesque feeling for the light face against the dark hair, the lighter gray background, the isolation of the red framing collar at the neck, the movement from gray to black at the top, the complexity of top (hair and comb pattern) and bottom (flowered kimono), the white hand blending in an unbroken way into the face so that it becomes one shape. This is extremely abstract. The ideas in my work may be different—for example, in a painting that moves from red to blue in nine stages—but I'm concerned with those relationships and thinking abstractly of that idea. But here Sharaku is too. Look at how the eyes stand out—everything is played down for that effect." Other adjectives he uses in connection with Japanese prints are also revealing of Anuszkiewicz's outlook—

46

47

"elegance," for example. "The Japanese have elegance even in their pornography, compared to other cultures."

He says of William Hogarth's black-and-white etching and engraving *Gin Lane* (plate 48): "I don't care for it. I do like Piranesi's engravings, however, his architectural style, particularly the prison series. They're more structured, more definite than this Hogarth. The Hogarth is mere storytelling. He's much more concerned with what he's saying than how he's saying it. It's insufficiently structured as a picture. Bruegel is much better in organization and structure than this in crowded

48

46. Piet Mondrian. *Composition with Red,
Yellow, and Blue.* 1930. Oil on canvas,
20 1/16 × 20 1/16". Collection Mr. and Mrs.
Armand P. Bartos, New York

47. Toshusai Sharaku. *Segawa Tomisaburo in
Female Character.* 1794. Woodcut,
14 1/4 × 9 3/8". British Museum, London

48. William Hogarth. *Gin Lane.* 1750–51.
Etching and engraving, 14 3/16 × 12".
British Museum, London

scenes. There isn't enough consideration to the total picture.
Look at Rembrandt's group scenes for example: he, too, is very
aware of the total composition. It's not just the overall grayness
and lack of contrast in this Hogarth—it's simply not interesting
in its abstract totality."

Anuszkiewicz's comments on these paintings and prints
show his preference for tightly structured compositions, intellectual art, simplicity, proportion, multiple repetitions, and the
interaction of color and shape. He sees his function as a painter
to be that of a planner and is happiest when he has maximum
control. It was to get greater control that he started using mechanical means of painting.

Does this mean that he never works with accidents or
randomness? Not absolutely. It has been mentioned earlier
that in his variables (plate 35) and trays (plate 36) he allows
the spectators to move the parts into their own arrangements,
even though he has his own preferred configurations. Further,
in reply to a question about possibility of spontaneity or happy
accidents in his painting Anuszkiewicz said in 1975: "My work
is almost architectural in technique. It's built, constructed so to
say, from the ground up. I have a conception, but as the painting develops physically—all through that process—I make
choices; the painting evolves in terms of those choices, which
are often spontaneous but not haphazard. At any given stage,
my perception determines what goes next. Even at the end I
have the option of change. No matter how much planning goes
into a work, reality is the act of painting. You can't foreknow the
result. In that sense accident is always possible."[33]

A summation of Anuszkiewicz's technique was offered in
1969 by one of his long-time observers: "Mr. Anuszkiewicz, in
spite of what appears to be his totally impersonal, hyperme-
thodical way of working, is a sensitive artist."[34]

Is Anuszkiewicz an Op painter? Today he does not see himself as such, and at the beginning of his professional career he did not foresee that the interest he was pursuing in his own work would become identified as "Op art."

Certain of his stylistic qualities are inherent in Suprematism, Constructivism, and de Stijl, specifically: (1) a use of simple geometric shapes: preeminently the square, the circle, and the rectangle; (2) an arrangement or calculation that frequently divides the picture surface in a mathematically precise manner; (3) a knowledge and use of the interaction of complementary colors, indicating an awareness of nineteenth-century precedents begun by scientists such as Michel-Eugène Chevreul and painters such as Georges Seurat; (4) an avoidance of deep perspective devices and an awareness of the picture surface, or the picture as object; (5) a direct perceptual appeal, free of emotive, symbolic, and commonly associative factors; (6) an anonymous, smooth, or impersonal surface. Those six characteristics were shared by most Op painters.

Beyond those characteristics, the artists identified with Op diverged sharply. Many of them were involved with serial configurations and periodic structures that were composed not of simple shapes but irregular or organic in form. The calculation of the picture may have been precise and yet have produced an effect of chaos, involving virtual or actual movement; in other words, stability was seldom the goal. Complementary colors may have been used, but some Op artists worked only in black and white, while others were involved in simultaneous, successive, or mixed contrast of colors. Some Op artists employed perspective devices that distorted the picture surface so that it appeared to heave or bulge, have concavities or convexities. Some of the painters were concerned with surface only to produce a dazzling or disconcerting retinal experience. And some preferred an anonymous surface not for maximum sensory experience but for ideological, even political, reasons—to change painting from an aristocratic art for the aesthetic few into one intended to reach as wide and untutored an audience as possible.

It was the fate of a number of artists in the early 1960s, each in his own way attracted toward geometric abstraction and psychological color investigation or space illusionism, to be lumped together under a label convenient to contemporary exhibitors or critics. Some of these "Op artists" have passed from the public view. Others, among them Richard Anuszkiewicz, have gone their separate ways. In Anuszkiewicz's work the necessity for geometric hard edge is clear. Strong optical effects can be achieved by a simple black-and-white confrontation: the contrast is maximal, completely clear, simple, and dramatic. But when the painting is in color, as Anuszkiewicz prefers, the need for a sharp, hard edge arises from the fact that color interaction takes place primarily where the colors meet, along a line or at the edges of a form.

Because of this, changes of scale can either destroy or enhance the painting. Each work is appropriate in size to the desired effect: a small work could not arbitrarily be enlarged without changing the effect. Also, since scale is so important, the reduction of paintings to a uniform scale in reproduction aids comprehension but destroys the effect of the original work.

Anuszkiewicz is not interested in actual movement, either motorized or computer-generated; nor is he interested in enlisting the spectator's own movement, as in some works with corrugated surfaces that produce two primary and several multiple effects. He does not work with afterimages, moiré effects, or light mechanisms.

However, he is concerned with movement of the starlike, streaming sort found in such demonstrations of optical illusion as the often-reproduced McKay figure (a black-and-white diagram of tapered rays converging toward the white center of a circle), suggesting an electromagnetic field, as in *Luminous* (1965, plate 49). He is also concerned with gentle apparent movement resulting from the composition alone, movement that may be perceived as flowing, advancing, or receding.

To induce this kind of movement, Anuszkiewicz employs a regular, uninterrupted structure providing a homogeneous surface of a periodic nature (a repeated overall structure) that prevents the eye from coming to rest in any one spot. The eye moves, unable to find any configuration that does not compete with another. This is the optical nature of the structure. There is much more than a simple principle of figure and ground at work here.

In Op paintings that juxtapose complementary colors of equal saturation the eye seeks to resolve the figure-ground relationship and cannot; the result is a fluctuation between figure and ground, producing a throbbing quality as each color seems to assert itself, or, more accurately, as the brain attempts to interpret the information received by the eye. Since there is no simplest solution, the effect is ambiguous and, because of this, immensely stimulating to some observers, immensely disturbing to others.

In paintings with overall modular structures, the complexity is increased, since the identical repetition of form means that no one form predominates. In this area Anuszkiewicz has

49. *Luminous.* 1965. Acrylic on Masonite, 24 × 24″. Collection Mr. and Mrs. Melvin Hirsch, Beverly Hills, Calif.

carried his experiments far beyond problems of interaction of color. His paintings are, in fact, static entities; but they appear to move. In reality, it is the eye of the observer that moves, able to focus only on small sections at a time.

In *Union of the Four* (1963, plate 50) Anuszkiewicz is not interested in successive contrast or afterimages. (One can easily test the after-image effect by staring fixedly at a red square and then shifting one's gaze to a blank white ground. The after-image appears as a square of green—the complementary color.) What takes place with this painting is mixed contrast (on a colored ground), in which adjacent colors assume a tinge of their complementaries. Here a grid of three colors—pale blue, blue-green, and yellow-green—overlies a uniform red ground, resulting in four distinct diamond shapes in the center and a number of shifting triangles in each corner.

Only in a few instances has Anuszkiewicz employed a pattern that gives the illusion of depth, for example *Knowledge and Disappearance* (1961, plate 51). But such illusions are atypical. Anuszkiewicz works with figure-ground and his space normally is the fluctuating, ambiguous one of alternation of front-back movement.

The ordinary figure-ground relationship (either a deep perspective space or the advancing space of Cubism) is not generally his concern, nor is simple figure-ground ambiguity. The virtual movement in his work is one of the chief differences between Anuszkiewicz's Op art and nonfigurative abstraction, which preceded it in this century. It creates a new kind of pictorial space depending—optically—not upon formal elements in the picture alone but upon the inability of the eye to organize and interpret the information received by it.

His new space is accompanied by a new light. One cannot

50. *Union of the Four.* 1963. Oil on canvas, 52 1/4 × 50 1/4″. Collection Mrs. Susan Morse Hilles, Old Lyme, Conn.

51. *Knowledge and Disappearance.* 1961. Oil
    on canvas, 50 × 49″. Philadelphia Museum of Art
    (purchase, the Beatrice Pastorius
    Kirner Fund)

judge distance or proximity in his paintings, since the colors and lines seem to hover, advance, and retreat tremulously. Thus the paintings appear to glow, as if they received more illumination than the adjacent wall. This incandescence is generated by maintaining the purity of each color and by utilizing the brilliance of acrylic paint, which permits a harder edge than oils. It is the shock of the optical color mix at the edge which produces the brilliance. In this sense, Anuszkiewicz's paintings are visual equivalents of certain kinds of energy—heat, light, electromagnetic force—or the sensations aroused by these phenomena. But his range is wide, and he has as much interest in the cool and somnolent as in the fiery and dazzling. His paintings are intellectual statements about sensation. This is not so contradictory as it might seem, since intellect is our sole gauge of sensation. The eye is more a seeking than a recording device—highly selective and as varied as the beholder himself.

Op art is direct and requires little previous knowledge of art. Children, as Anuszkiewicz has noted, delight in it. Other viewers are aware of formal structure, relationships, and complexities but are just as delighted. This art appeals on as many levels as there are levels of awareness and experience. It depends upon the viewer's expectations whether he is pleased or dissatisfied with an artist's work. If the observer wishes to find confirmation of his own preconceptions, he may look at the work of an experimental artist with indifference, disappointment, or even animosity. If, on the other hand, the spectator is open to surprise, to a new facet or interpretation, to a wholly unexpected transformation of what is known, he may find in the artist's presentation a revelation surpassing his anticipations.

That the public prefers figurative to nonfigurative painting is well known. That it should have found pleasure in Op painting can mean only that a direct response was felt, and this is communication.

Anuszkiewicz has said: "The ideas I work with are essentially timeless. If you're working with present-day subject matter, your work can grow old and unimportant. Working with basic ideas will always be exciting, and if a color or form is visually exciting in any profound sense, it will be that way ten or twenty years from now also."

He was the first Op artist on the American scene. In today's art world, being first can be a matter of minutes, so that it is of no great importance. What does matter is that when the movement waned he continued to grow and develop. He now commands attention as one of America's most distinguished solitary painters.

NOTES

Quotations from Richard Anuszkiewicz, unless otherwise noted, are from the author's discussions with the artist.

1. United States Information Service, *Anuszkiewicz* (cat.), Washington, D.C., 1974

2. *Art News,* October, 1967, Vol. 66, No. 6, "Reviews and Previews," p. 12

3. *Art News,* May, 1975, Vol. 74, No. 5, "New York Reviews," pp. 98–99

4. Jay Jacobs, "Portrait of the Artist," *the-ARTgallery,* March, 1971, Vol. XIV, No. 6, p. 33

5. *The New York Times,* Feb. 21, 1965, Sec. 2, p. 19

6. *Ibid.*

7. The Contemporaries, which closed in 1966, was a gallery located at 992 Madison Avenue, New York.

8. Carlyle Burrows, " 'Scientific' Designs," *New York Herald Tribune,* April 8, 1961

9. Stuart Preston, "Slight of Eye," *The New York Times,* April 2, 1961

10. *Ibid.*

11. Burrows, *op cit.*

12. *Ibid.*

13. Stuart Preston, " 'Les Animaliers' Stage Comeback," *The New York Times,* March 4, 1963

14. John Gruen, " 'Americans 1963' at Modern Museum," *New York Herald Tribune,* May 22, 1963; repeated in "The Trend of the Times in Modern Art," *New York Herald Tribune,* May 23, 1963

15. John Gruen, "Pop Goes the Easel," *New York Herald Tribune,* May 26, 1963

16. Miles A. Smith, "Pop Art Losing Its Shock Appeal?," *Daily American,* July 4, 1963

17. *Time,* Oct. 23, 1964

18. *Life,* Dec. 28, 1964

19. Grace Glueck, "Blues and Greens on Reds," *The New York Times,* Feb. 21, 1965; also John Canaday, "Optics Are the Stalk of the Town," *The New York Times,* Jan. 30, 1965

20. Hilton Kramer, "Clashing Values of 2 Generations," *The New York Times,* Nov. 6, 1965

21. Sidney Tillim, "Optical Art: Pending or Ending?," *Arts Magazine,* January, 1965, p. 23

22. Barbara Rose, "Beyond Vertigo: Optical Art at the Modern," *Artforum,* April, 1965, p. 31

23. Lucy Lippard, "Perverse Perspectives," *Art International,* March 20, 1967, p. 28

24. Tillim, *op. cit.,* p. 22

25. R. Buckminster Fuller and Robert Marks, *The Dymaxion World of Buckminster Fuller,* Anchor Press/Doubleday, Garden City, N.Y., 1973, p. 58

26. Françoise Henry, *Irish Art in the Early Christian Period, to 800 A.D.,* Ithaca, N.Y., Cornell University Press, 1965, pp. 205–8

27. Thomas Burnet, *Telluris Theoria Sacra: Orbis Nostri Originem et Mutationes Generalis . . .,* London, 1681; English trans. *The Sacred Theory of the Earth . . .,* London, 1684. The quotation is from 6th ed. reprinted 1965, Southern Illinois University Press, Carbondale, Ill., Book II, Chapter xi, p. 220.

28. Grace Glueck, *The New York Times,* Feb. 21, 1965

29. The three *Convex & Concave* pieces, numbered I, II, and III in the Sidney Janis exhibition catalogue of 1967, were not executed in that order (number III actually being first), but the numbers assigned to them in that catalogue have been followed here.

30. *Art in America,* March-April, 1970, p. 56

31. *The Sunday Home News,* New Brunswick, N.J., Oct. 8, 1972

32. John Canaday, *The New York Times,* Sept. 16, 1972

33. *Recent Paintings* (cat.), Andrew Crispo Gallery, New York, 1975, conversation with Gene Baro

34. John Canaday, *The New York Times,* April 5, 1969

PLATES

52

53

55

54

52. *From My Kitchen Window.* 1945.
    Watercolor, 14 × 21".
    Collection the artist

53. *Church Across the Street at
    Christmas.* 1946. Watercolor,
    15 1/2 × 19 1/2".
    Collection the artist

54. *Backyard.* 1946. Watercolor and
    oil on gesso panel, 18 × 24".
    Collection the artist

55. *Chewing the Rag.* 1946.
    Watercolor and oil on gesso
    panel, 12 1/2 × 17 1/2".
    Collection the artist

56. *Bonfire.* 1946.
    Watercolor, 15 1/2 × 19 1/2".
    Collection the artist

56

57

58

59

60

61

57. *Between Two Houses*. 1949.
Oil on Masonite, 24 × 36″.
Collection the artist

58. *Afternoon Shadows*. 1947. Watercolor,
14 1/2 × 19″. Collection the artist

59. *Monday Morning*. 1947. Watercolor and
oil on gesso panel, 12 × 17″.
Collection the artist

60. Untitled. 1947. Watercolor,
15 1/2 × 19 1/2″. Collection the artist

61. Untitled. 1947. Watercolor,
15 1/2 × 19 1/2″. Collection the artist

62. *Negro Wedding*. 1949. Watercolor
and oil on gesso panel, 29 1/2 × 40″.
Collection the artist

62

63. *Cellar Still Life.* 1949. Pencil,
13 3/4 × 10 1/2″. Collection the artist

64. *Butterfly Boy.* 1950. Egg tempera on panel, 13 × 33″. Collection the artist

65. *Woman in White*. 1950. Tempera on board,
    29 3/4 × 19 3/4″. Collection the artist

66. *The Bridge*. 1950. Tempera on board,
    24 1/4 × 17 1/4″. Collection the artist

67. *Still Life with Pears.* 1951. Oil on Masonite, 24 × 36″. Collection the artist

68

69

70

68. *Tom.* 1953. Oil on canvas, 32 × 27″.
Collection the artist

69. *Kolbe Fisheries.* 1951. Oil on Masonite, 28 × 38″.
Collection the artist

70. *The Artist.* 1951. Oil on Masonite, 25 1/2 × 30 1/2″.
Collection the artist

71. Untitled. 1954. Pencil, 15 × 9″.
Collection the artist

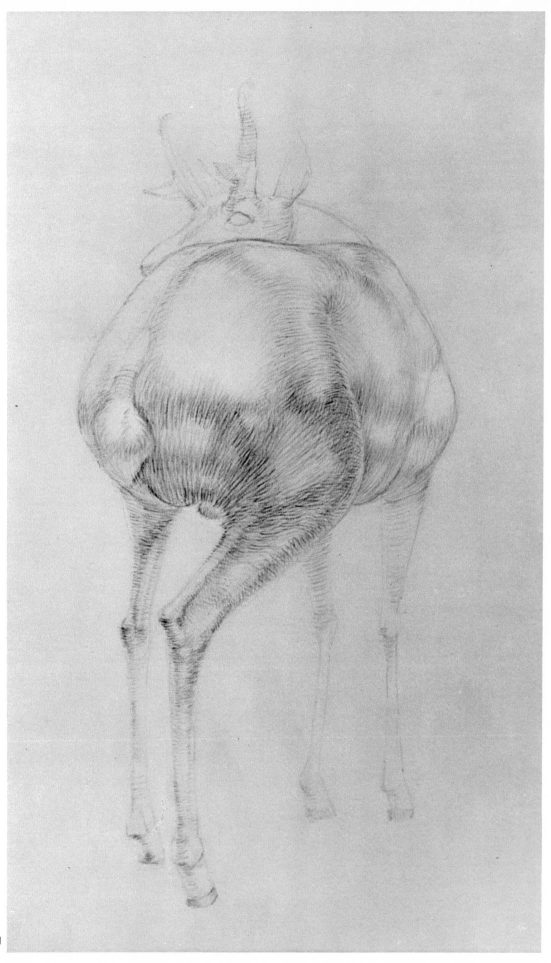

72. *People Leaving*. 1954. Watercolor and oil
on gesso panel, 19 1/2 × 31″. Collection the artist

73. *Self-portrait*. 1954. Oil on canvas and
wood panel, 21 × 14″. Collection the artist

74. *Gold and Green.* 1955. Tempera and oil on board, 40 1/2 × 30″. Collection the artist

75. *Blue on Orange.* 1955. Tempera on board, 40 1/2 × 30″. Collection the artist

76. Untitled. 1956. Watercolor, 18 × 21 1/2″. Collection the artist

77. *Red on Silver.* 1955. Tempera and oil on board, 30 × 40 1/2″. Collection the artist

74

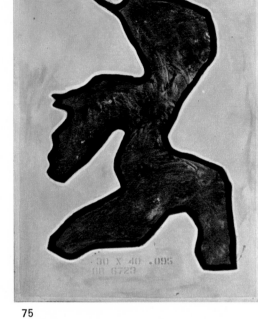

75

76

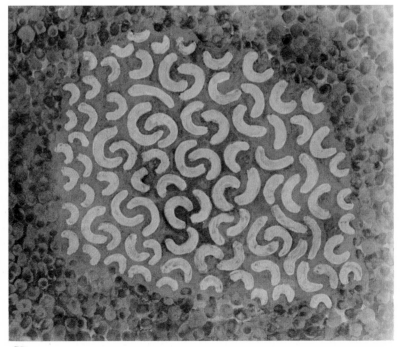

77

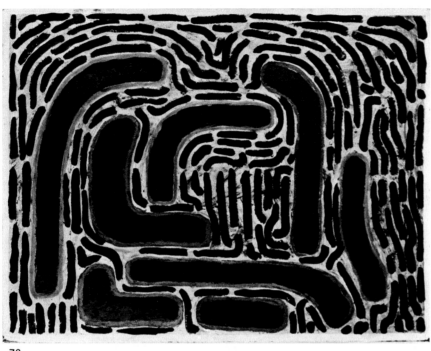

78

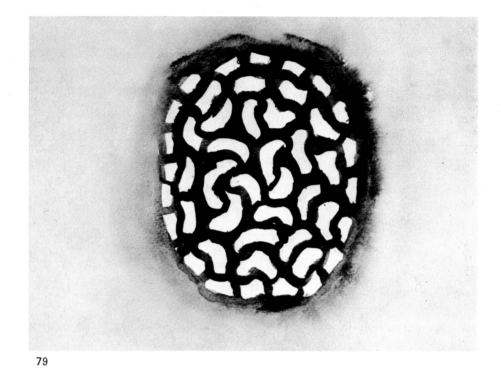

79

80

81

78. Untitled. 1956. Watercolor, 18 × 21″.
Collection the artist

79. *White Shapes.* 1956. Watercolor,
10 1/2 × 14 1/2″. Collection the artist

80. *Red and Green Reversed.* n.d. Oil
on canvas, 20 × 16″. Collection the artist

81. *Yellow on Silver.* 1956.
Watercolor with silver paint, 18 × 21 1/2″.
Collection the artist

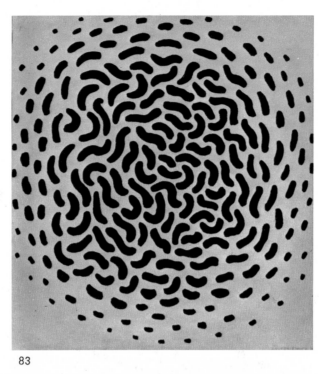

82

83

82. *Warm on Cool*, 1956.
Watercolor, 14 1/2 × 10 1/2".
Collection the artist

83. *Concentric.* 1957. Oil on canvas,
30 × 28". Collection the artist

84. *Fire Ball.* 1956. Tempera and oil on board,
9 1/2 × 20 1/2". Collection the artist

85. Untitled. 1957. Oil on canvas,
32 × 28". Collection the artist

86. *Green and Red, Figure and Ground.* 1956.
Oil on canvas, 32 × 40". Collection the artist

87. *Blue Center.* 1957. Oil on canvas,
20 × 29". Collection the artist

88. *Break-up.* 1957. Oil on canvas, 45 1/2 × 33 1/2".
Collection the artist

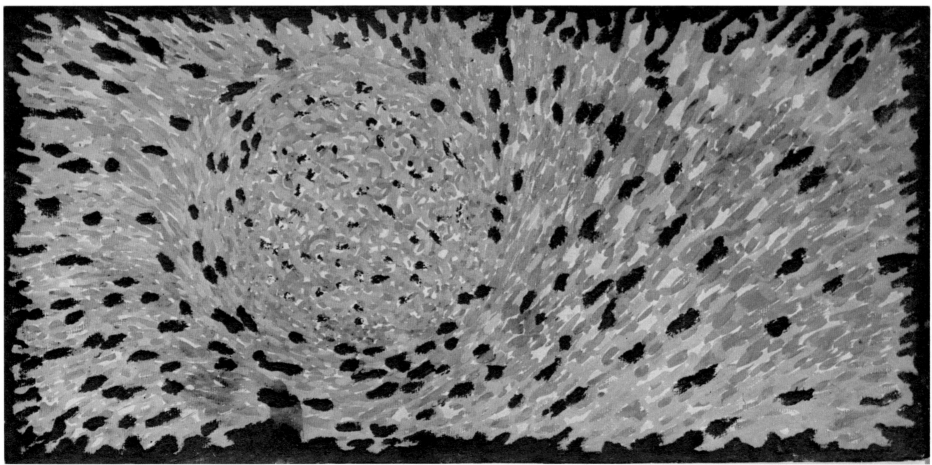

84

85

87

86

88

89. *Nude.* 1957. Pencil, 13 1/4 × 10".
    Collection the artist

90. *Male Nude.* 1957. Pencil, 13 3/4 × 9 1/2".
    Collection the artist

89

90

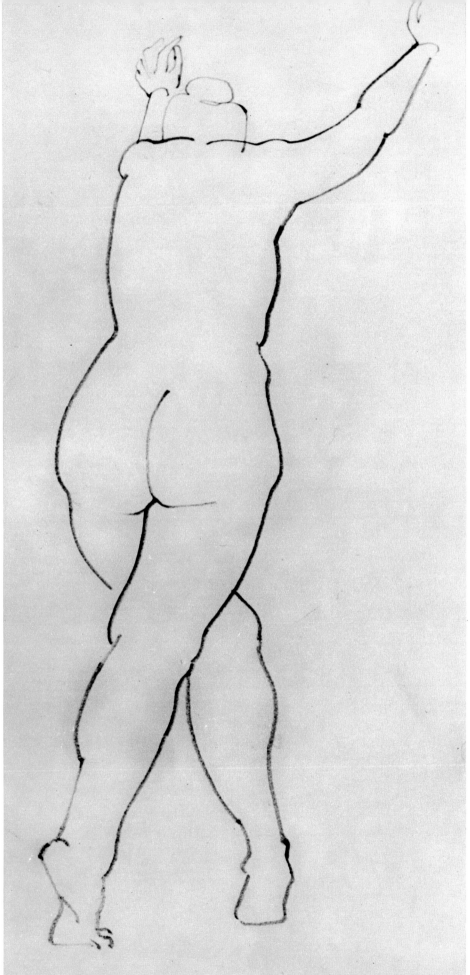

91. *Female Nude.* 1957. Pencil, 13 × 9".
Collection the artist

92. Untitled. 1957. Pencil, 13 × 9 1/2".
Collection the artist

91

92

93

94

95

93. *On Blue.* 1957. Watercolor, 22 × 26″.
Collection the artist

94. Untitled. 1957. Watercolor, 22 × 25 1/2″.
Collection the artist

95. *Green on Red.* 1957. Tempera on board,
17 1/2 × 26″. Collection the artist

96. Untitled. 1958. Ink, 9 1/2 × 8″.
Collection the artist

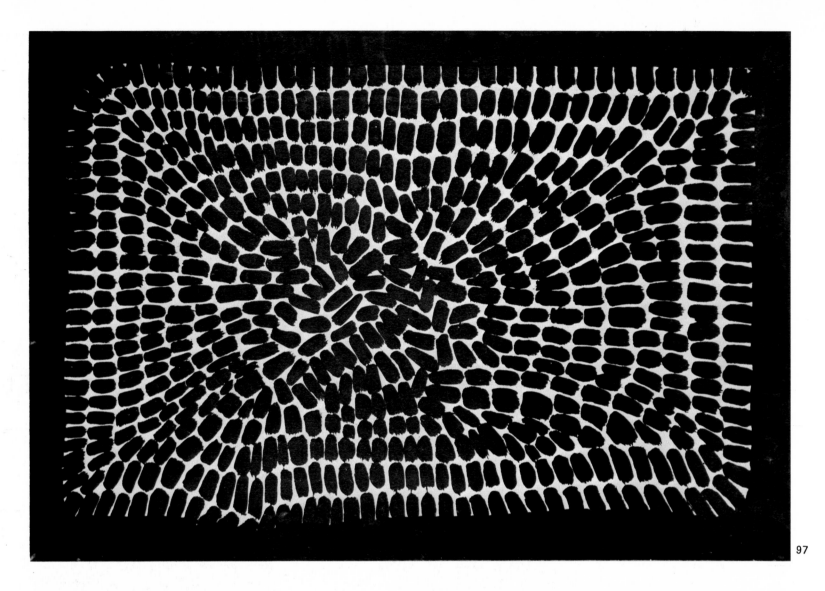

97

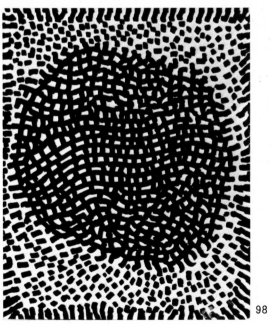

98

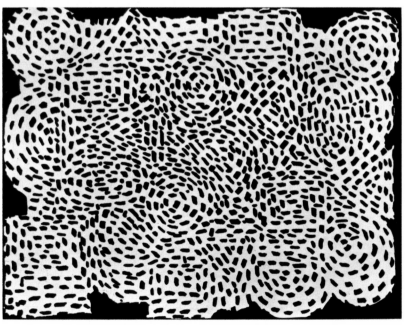

99

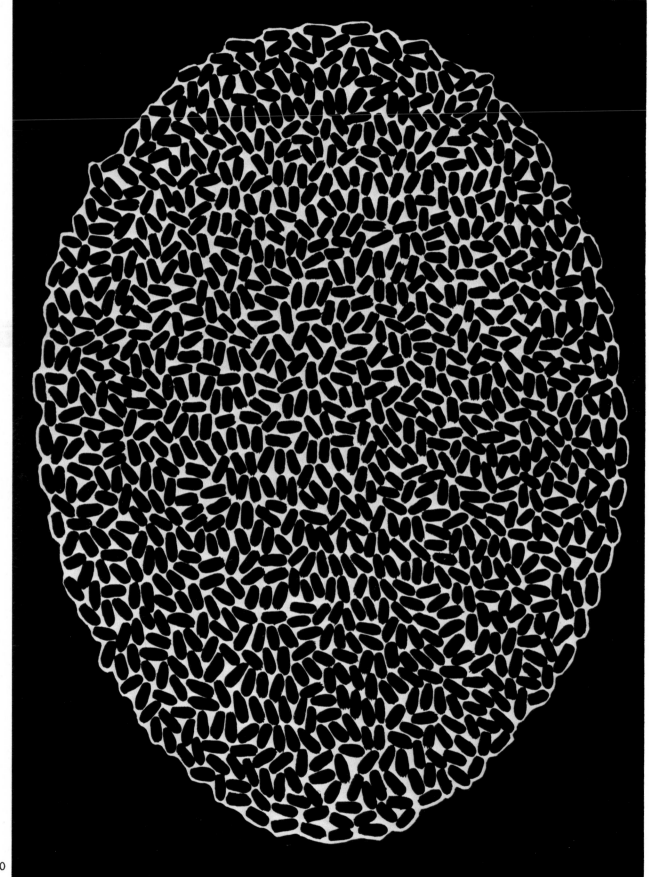

97. *Seventh Authority.* 1958. Oil on
canvas. Collection Mr. and Mrs.
Henry Feiwel, Larchmont, N.Y.

98. Untitled. 1958. Ink, 7 3/8 × 6″.
Collection the artist

99. Untitled. 1958. Ink, 6 × 8″.
Collection the artist

100. *Winter Recipe.* 1958. Oil on canvas,
48 × 36″. Collection Mr. and Mrs.
David Evins, New York

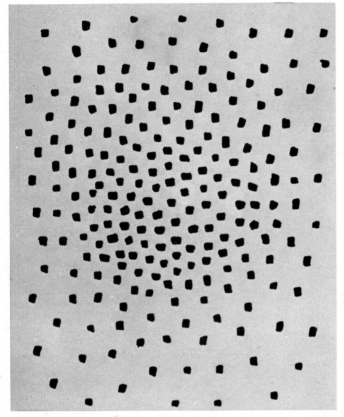

101

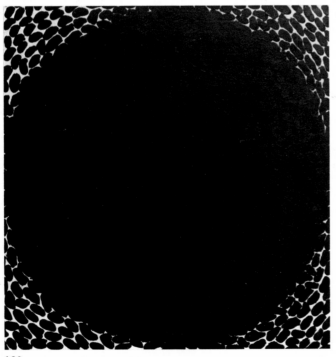

102

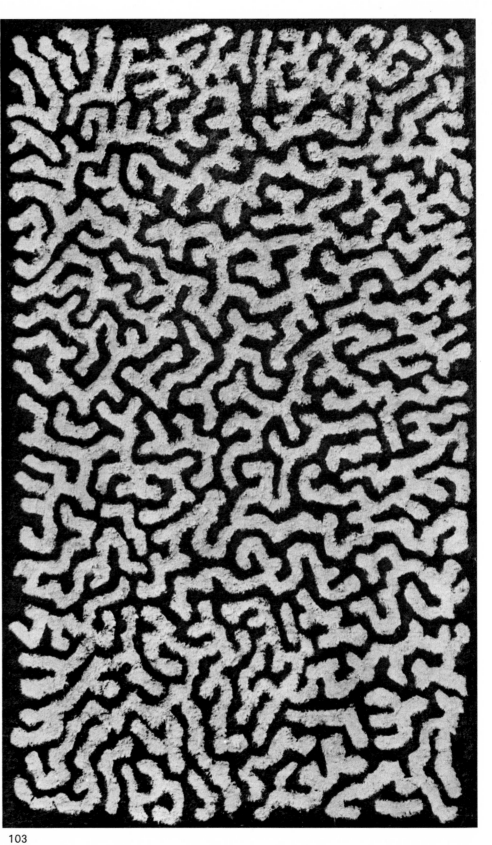

103

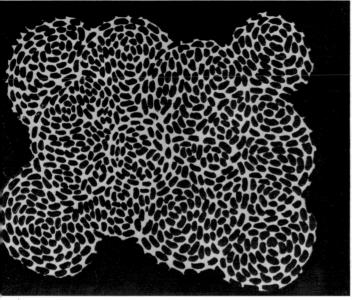

104

101. Untitled. 1958. Ink, 7 × 5 1/2".
Collection the artist

102. *Dark Center.* 1959. Oil on canvas,
26 × 26". Collection the artist

103. *Dissolving the Edge of Green.* 1959. Oil on
canvas, 22 × 13 1/2". Collection the artist

104. *Rising and Descending.* 1959. Oil on
canvas, 18 × 24". Collection the artist

105. *Emerald Tablet.* 1959. Oil on canvas,
36 × 28". Collection the artist

105

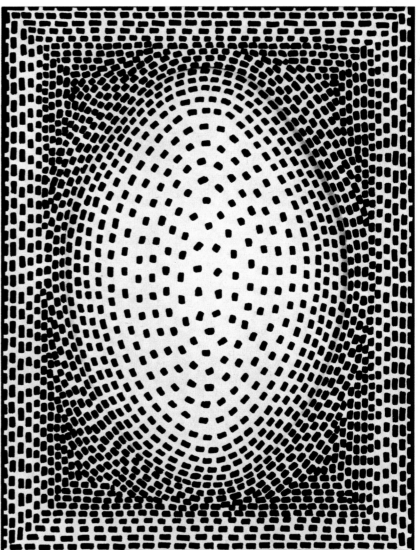

106. *Slow Center*. 1959. Oil on canvas, 36 × 33″. Collection the artist

107. Untitled. 1960. Ink. Collection the artist

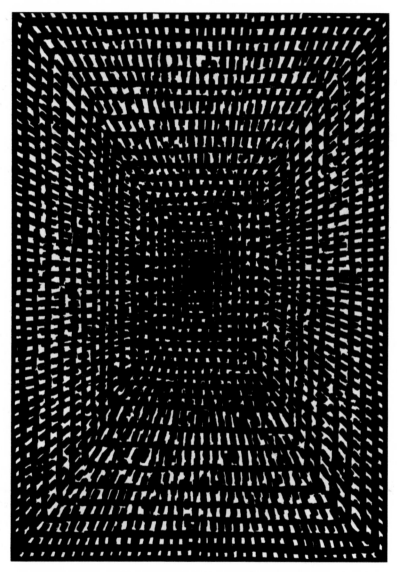

108. *The Vaulted World*. 1961. Oil on canvas, 50 × 45″.
Collection Theodore E. Stebbins, Jr., Cambridge, Mass.

109. *From the Center*. 1961. Ink, 10 3/4 × 7 3/4″.
Collection the artist

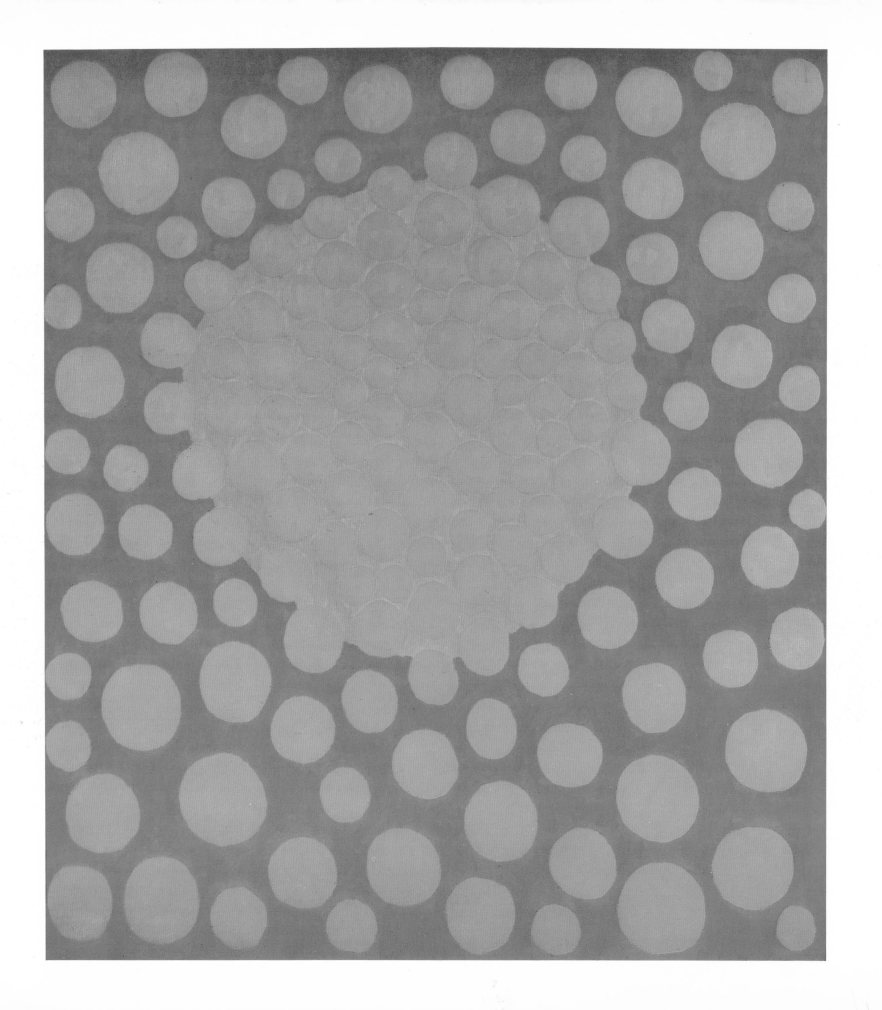

110. *Fluorescent Complement.* 1960. Oil on canvas, 36 × 32 1/4".
The Museum of Modern Art, New York (Larry Aldrich Foundation Fund)

111. *The Dual Privileges.* 1961. Oil on canvas, 54 × 54".
Collection Mr. and Mrs. Morton J. Hornick, New York

112. *The Burning Glass.* 1961. Oil on canvas, 54 1/4 × 50 1/8".
Collection William H. Burden, New York

113. *Triumphal Color.* 1960. Oil on canvas, 49 1/4 × 50″. Collection Michael Kan, Detroit

114. Untitled. 1962. Acrylic on Masonite, 24 × 22″. Collection Otto and Marguerite Nelson, New York

115. *Quadernity of the Cross in the Zodiac.* 1962. Oil on canvas, 42 × 40″.
Collection Mr. and Mrs. David Steine, Nashville, Tenn.

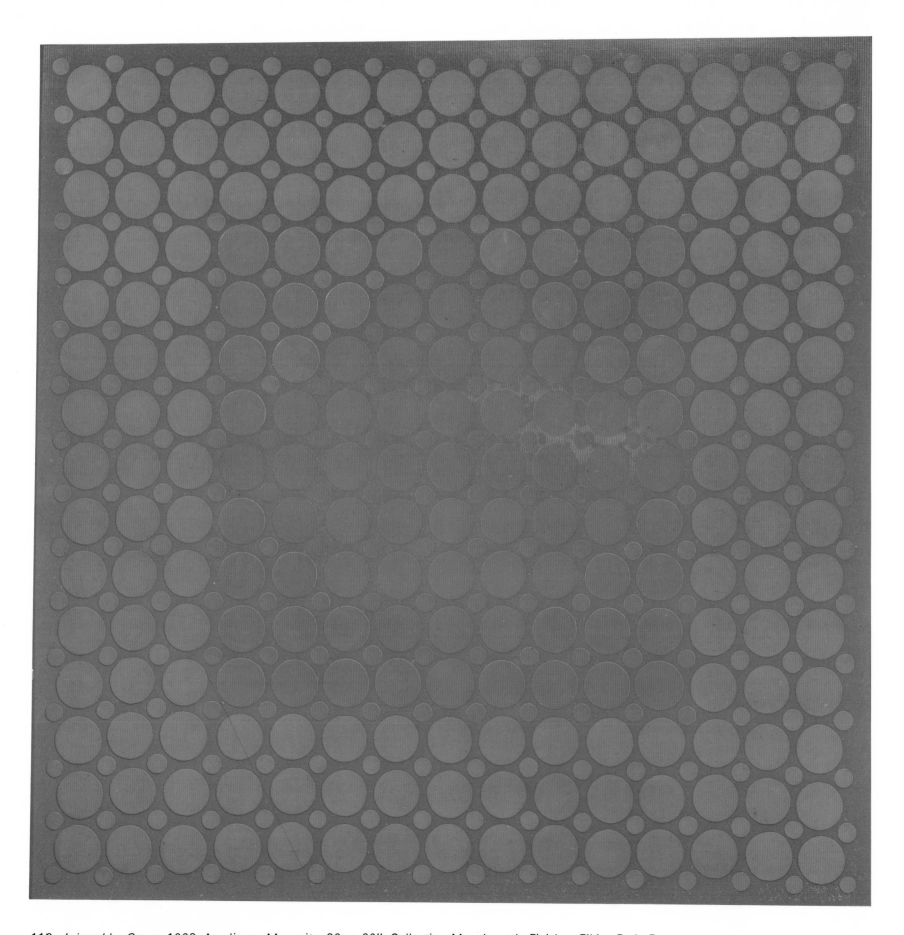

116. *Injured by Green.* 1963. Acrylic on Masonite, 36 × 36". Collection Mrs. Janet L. Fleisher, Elkins Park, Pa.

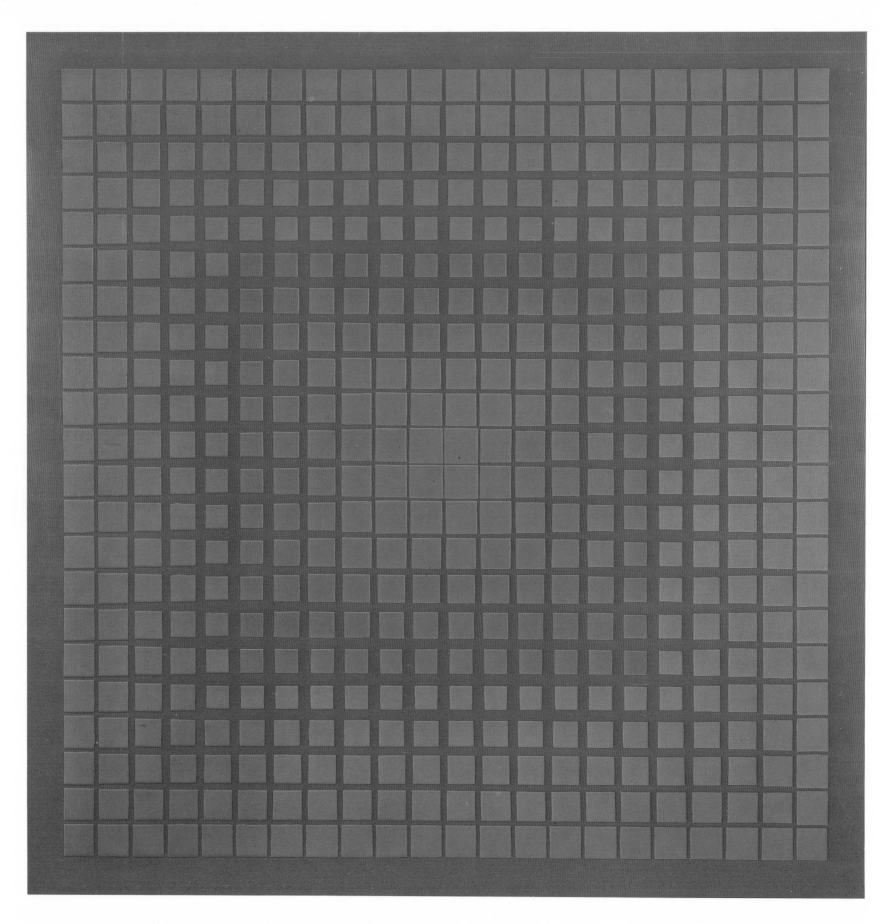

117. *The Fourth of the Three.* 1963. Acrylic on Masonite, 48 1/2 × 48 1/2". The Whitney Museum
of American Art, New York (gift of the Friends of the Whitney Museum)

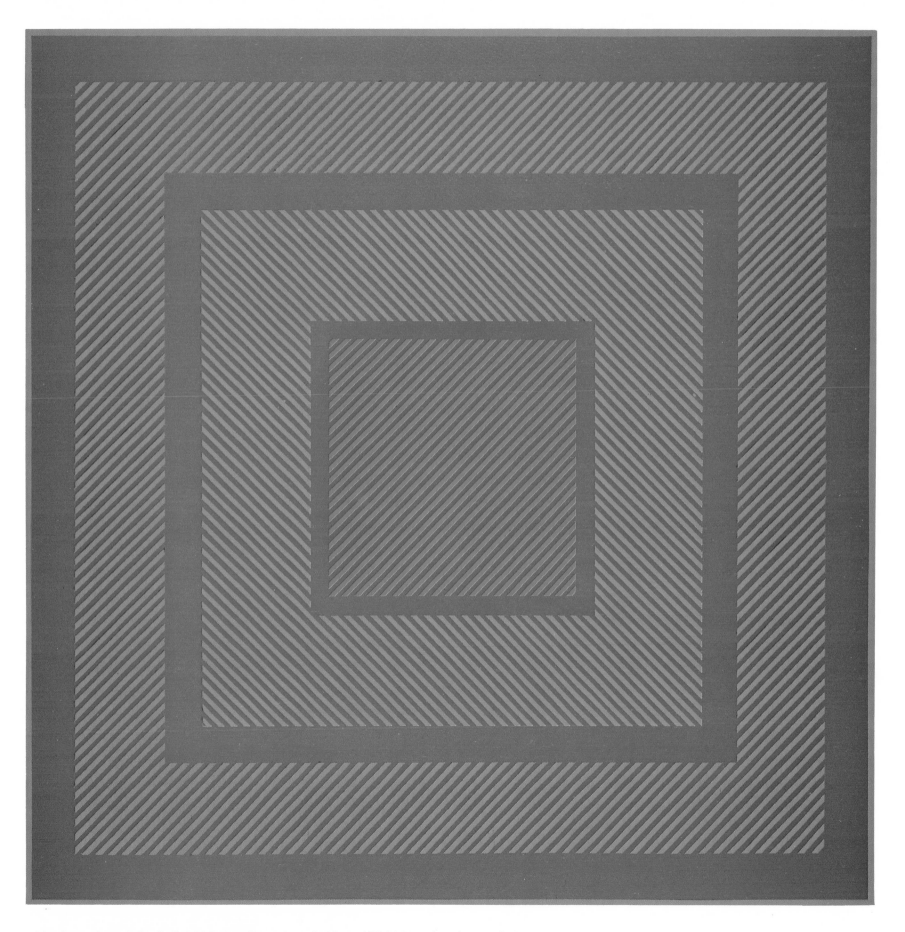

118. *Sounding of the Bell*. 1964. Acrylic on board, 48 × 48″. Yale University Art Gallery, New Haven
(gift of the artist under the Ford Foundation Purchase Fund)

119. *Water from the Rock*. 1961–62. Acrylic
on canvas, 50 × 52 1/2″. The Albright-Knox Art Gallery,
Buffalo, N.Y. (gift of Sumner H. Knox)

120. *Exact Quantity*. 1963. Acrylic on Masonite,
18 × 31″. The Larry Aldrich Museum of
Contemporary Art, Ridgefield, Conn.

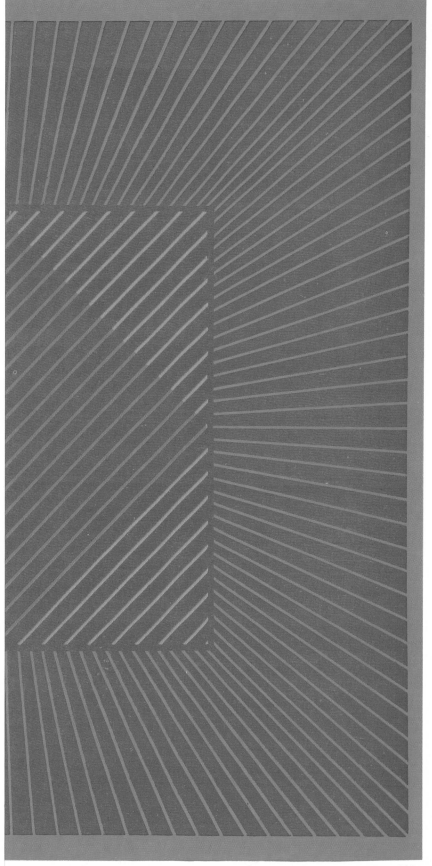

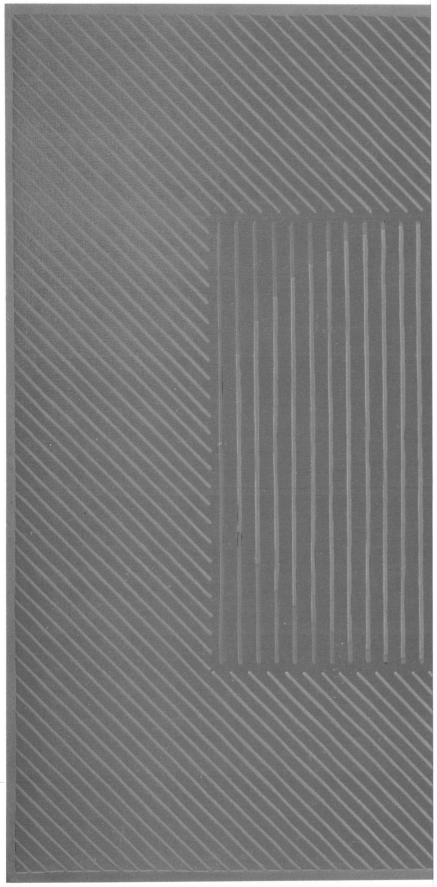

122. *Moon and Sun Furnaces.* 1963. Acrylic on panel, 48 × 48". Collection the artist

121. *The Two Equinoxes.* 1963. Acrylic on Masonite, 24 × 24". Collection Mr. and Mrs. David Steine, Nashville, Tenn.

123. *Bound Vapor*. 1964. Acrylic on Masonite, 30 × 30″. Collection Mr. and Mrs. John Heinz III.

124. *Complementary Fission*. 1964. Acrylic on Masonite, 48 × 48″. Albert A. List Family Collection, Byram, Conn.

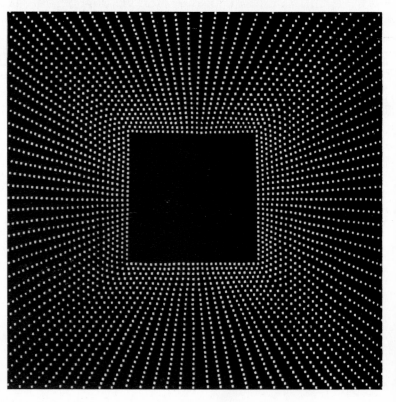

126. *Force of Light.* 1964. Acrylic on board, 24 × 24″.
Private collection

125. *Complementary Forces.* 1964. Oil on canvas, 20 × 15″.
Collection Mr. Phillip A. Bruno, New York

127. Rug. 1964. Painted on calfskin for Jacques Kaplan,
New York. 71 × 71″. La Jolla Museum of Contemporary Art,
La Jolla, Calif.

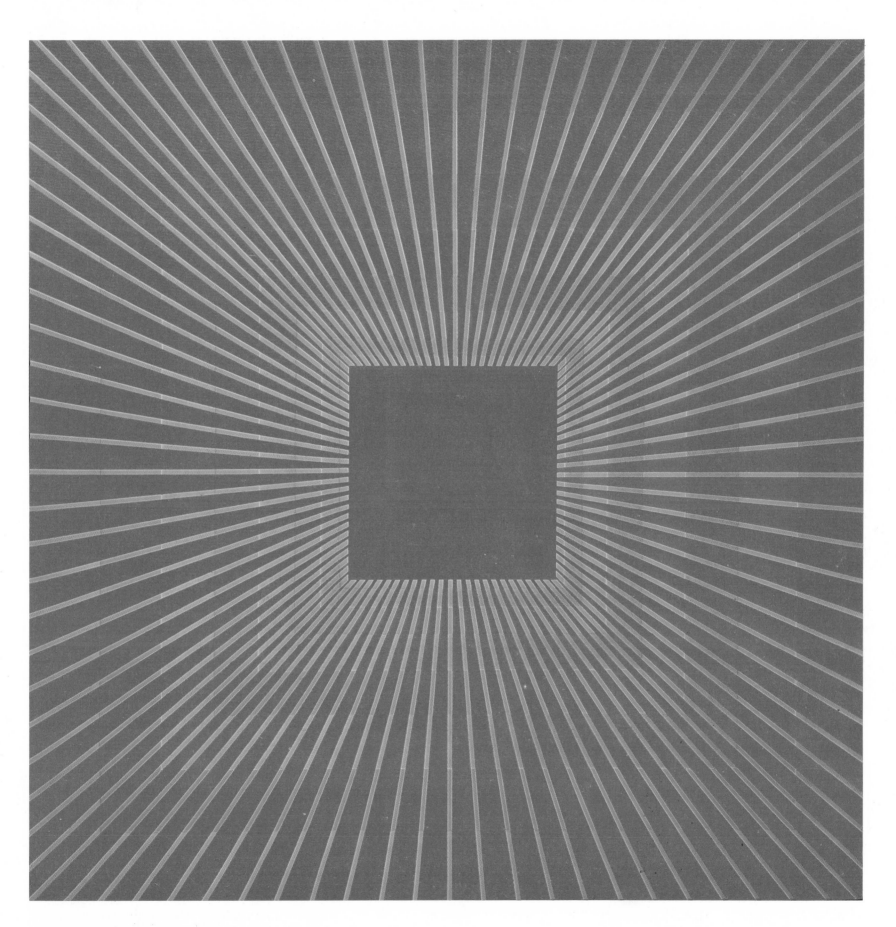

128. *Mercurian in the Fire*. 1964. Acrylic on Masonite, 48 × 48″. Collection Mr. and Mrs. Myron A. Minskoff, New York

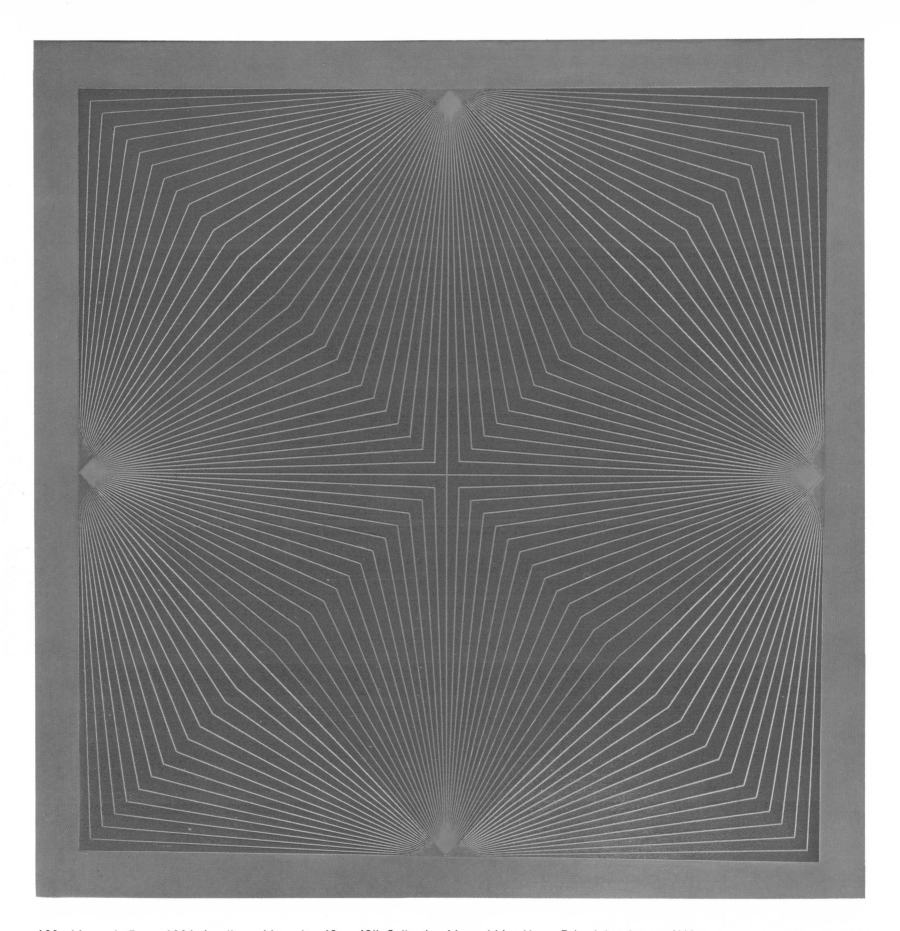

129. *Magnetic Force.* 1964. Acrylic on Masonite, 48 × 48″. Collection Mr. and Mrs. Henry Feiwel, Larchmont, N.Y.

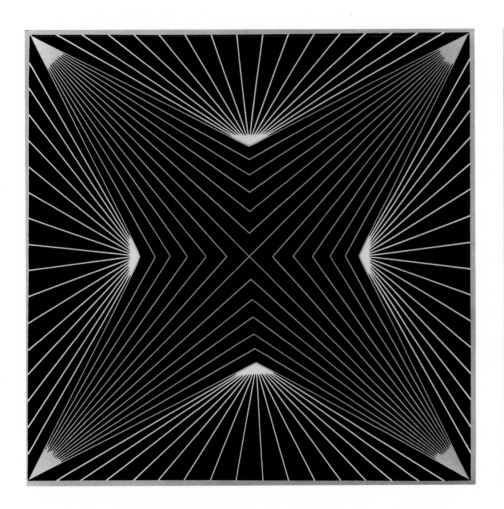

130. *Corona.* 1965. Acrylic on Masonite, 18 × 18″.
Collection Mrs. Stanley J. Sarnoff, Bethesda, Md.

131. *Radiant Green.* 1965. Acrylic on board, 16 × 16″. The Museum
of Modern Art, New York (Sidney and Harriet Janis Collection)

132. *Divisible*. 1965. Acrylic on Masonite, 36 × 36″.
Collection Mrs. Susan Morse Hilles, Old Lyme, Conn.

133. *Scintillant*. 1965. Acrylic on Masonite, 36 × 36″.
Collection Mr. and Mrs. Herman Elkon, New York

134. *Derived from Without.* 1965. Acrylic on canvas,
    66 × 66″. Collection Mr. and Mrs. A. I. Sherr, New York

135. *Progression: In and Out.* 1965. Acrylic on canvas,
    48 × 48″. Private collection

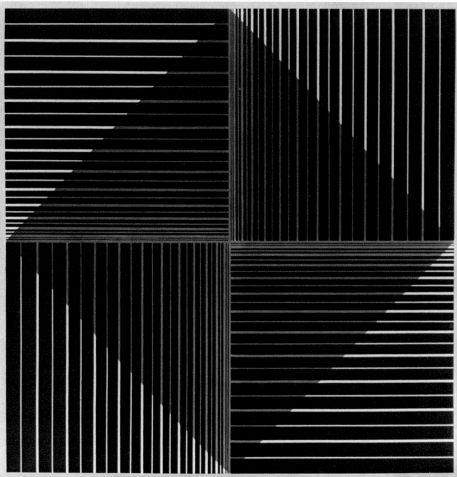

136. *Contained.* 1965. Acrylic on Masonite, 36 × 36″.
Collection Mr. and Mrs. Frank H. Porter, Cleveland

137. *Splitting the Red.* 1965. Acrylic on Masonite, 48 × 48″.
Private collection

138. *The Edge of All Activity.* 1965. Acrylic on canvas, 60 × 60″. The City Museum of St. Louis

139. *Inner Dichotomy*. 1965. Acrylic on
board, 36 × 36″. Private collection

140. *Intrinsic Harmony*. 1965. Acrylic on
board, 24 × 24″. Collection the artist

141. *Distinctness of Red*. 1965. Acrylic
on Masonite, 36 × 36″. Collection Srta.
Margarita Miller

142. *Iridescence*. 1965. Acrylic on canvas, 60 × 60″. The Albright-Knox Art Gallery, Buffalo, N.Y. (gift of Seymour H. Knox)

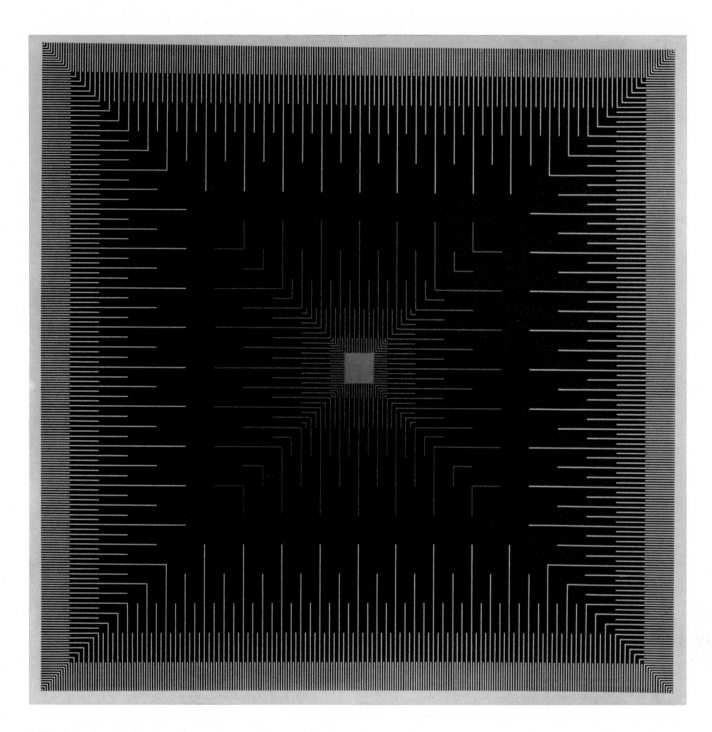

143. *Stimulus.* 1965. Acrylic on canvas, 72 × 72″. Collection the artist

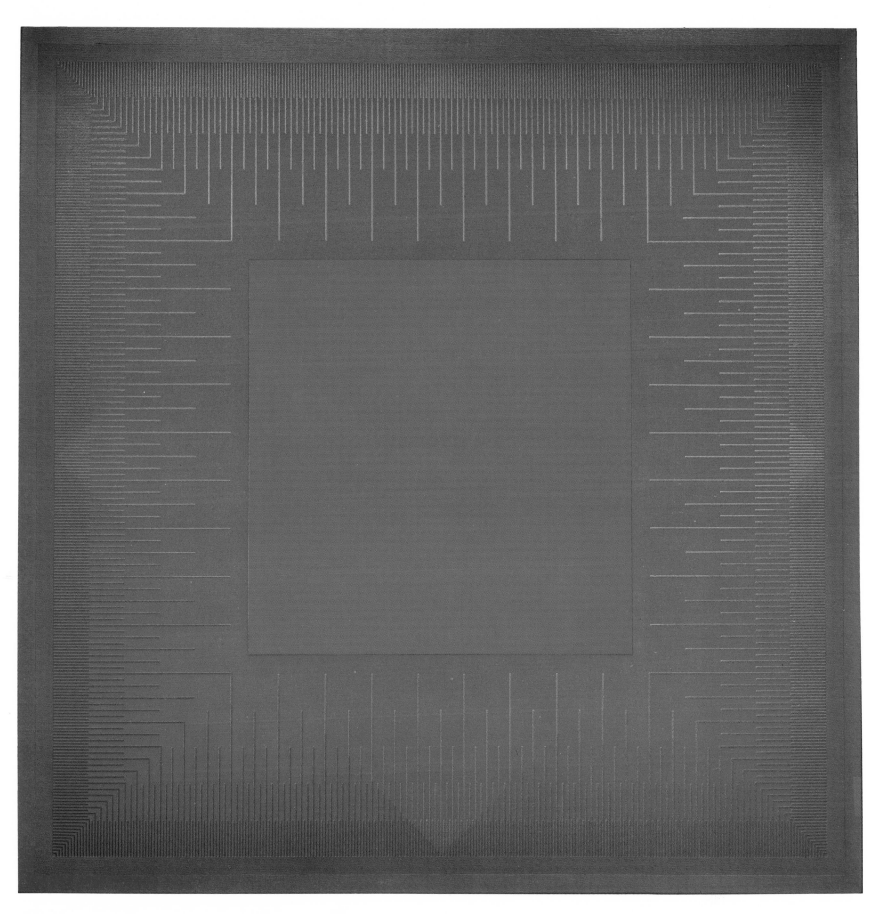

144. *Intensity*. 1965. Acrylic on canvas, 72 × 72″. Collection Mr. and Mrs. R. B. Mayer

145. *Crimson Sanctuary*. 1965. Acrylic on board, 36 × 36″. Collection the Honorable and Mrs. Burton Peskin, Princeton, N.J.

146. *Primary Contrast.* 1965. Acrylic on canvas, 60 × 60″. The Currier Gallery of Art, Manchester, N.H. (gift of the Saul O. Sidore Memorial Foundation)

147. *Between*. 1966. Acrylic on canvas, 84 × 84″. Dartmouth College Collection, Hanover, N.H.

148. *Apex*. 1966. Acrylic on canvas, 84 × 84″. Collection the artist

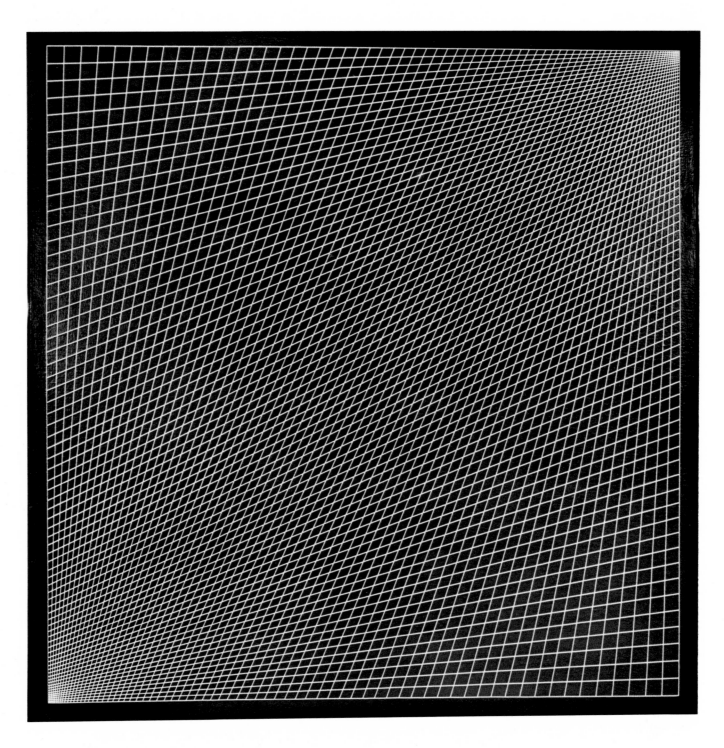

149. *One Quarter.* 1966. Acrylic on canvas, 60 × 60″. New Jersey State Museum, Trenton

150. *Splendor of Red*. 1965. Acrylic on canvas, 72 × 72″. Yale University Art Gallery, New Haven

151. *Sol I*. 1965. Acrylic on canvas, 84 × 84″. Hirshhorn Museum and Sculpture Garden, Washington, D.C.

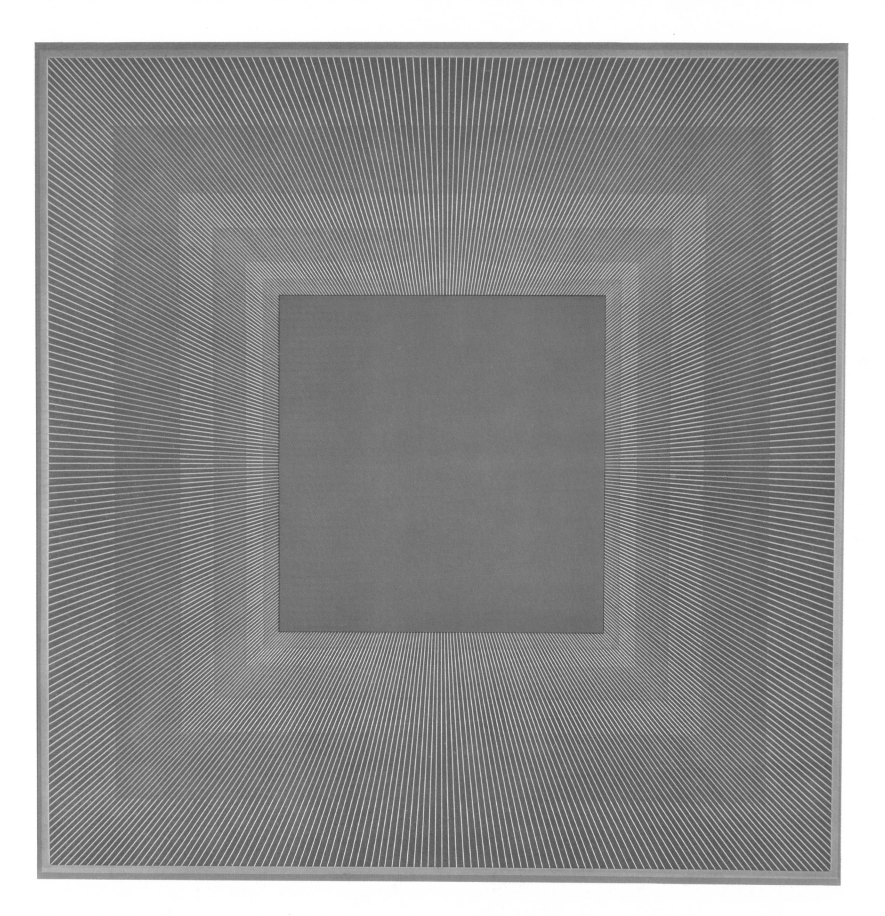

152. *Sol II*. 1965. Acrylic on canvas, 84 × 84″. The Milwaukee Art Center Collection (gift of the Friends of Art)

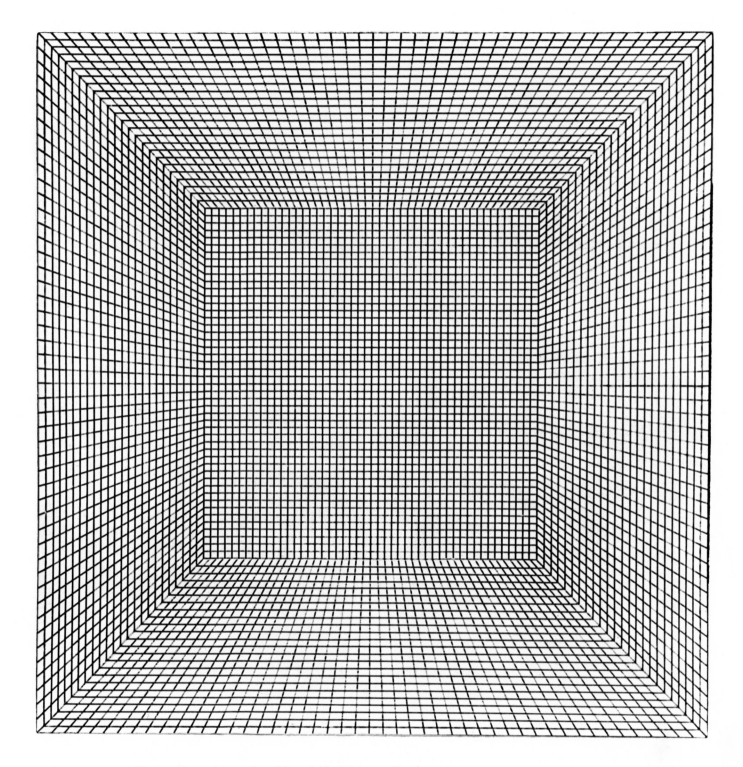

153. *Density.* 1966. Acrylic on Masonite, 24 × 24″. Private collection

154. *Visible State*. 1966. Acrylic on Masonite, 24 × 24″. Private collection

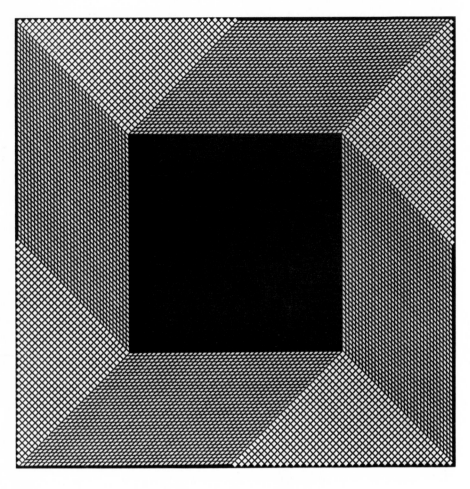

155. *Middle of All Activity.* 1966. Acrylic on
Masonite, 24 × 24″. Collection the artist

156. *Related Blue and Green.* 1965. Acrylic on Masonite, 36 × 48″.
Collection J. Daniel Weitzman, Hartsdale, N.Y.

157. *Inflexional II.* 1966. Acrylic on Masonite, 36 × 36″.
Collection the Chattanooga Art Association, Chattanooga, Tenn.

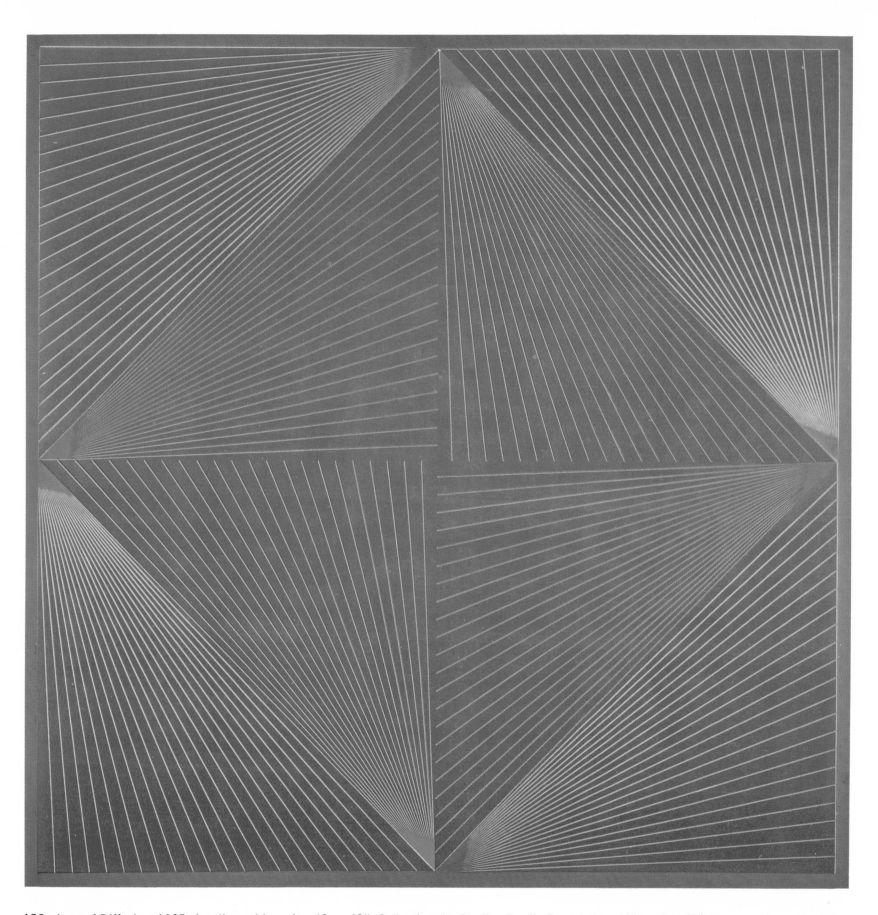

158. *Law of Diffusion*. 1965. Acrylic on Masonite, 48 × 48″. Collection the Bradley Family Foundation, Milwaukee, Wisc.

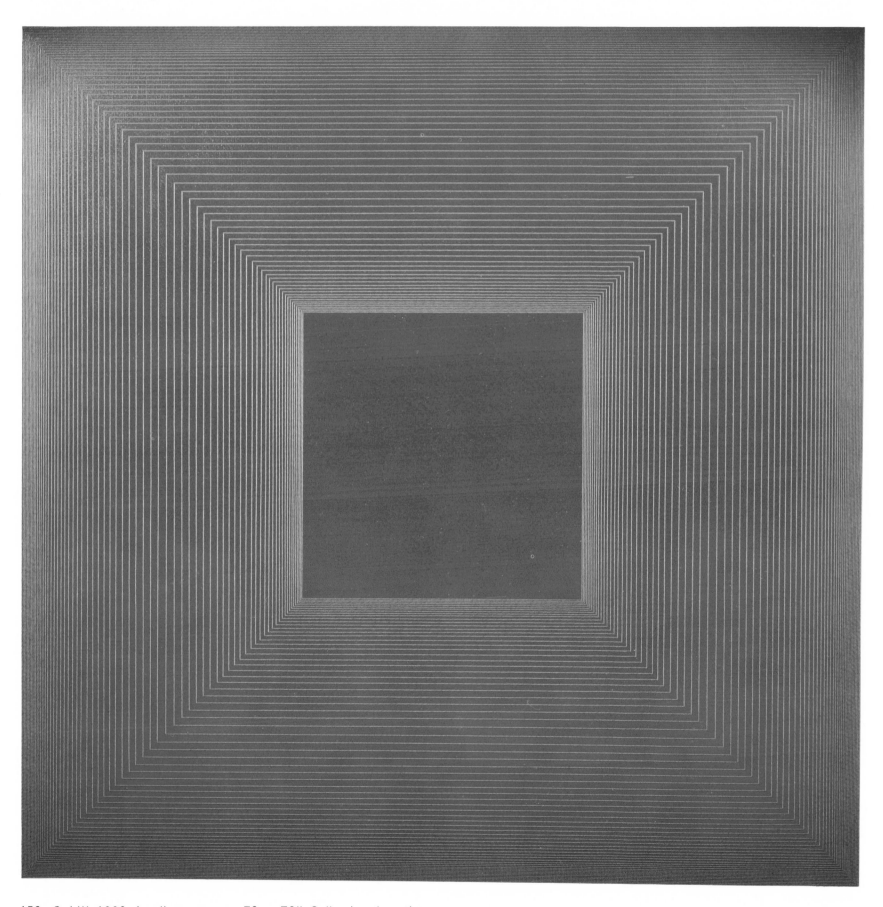

159. *Sol III*. 1966. Acrylic on canvas, 72 × 72″. Collection the artist

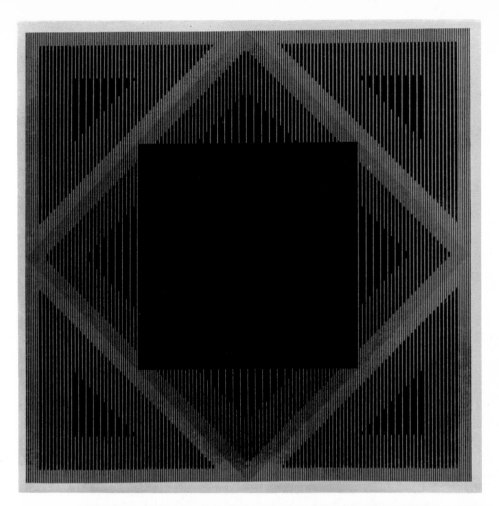

162. *Geometric*. 1966. Acrylic on Masonite, 36 × 36″. Collection the artist

163. *Celestial*. 1966. Acrylic on canvas, 60 × 60″. Collection the artist

164–68. *The Cadmiums.* 1966. Acrylic on Masonite, five panels, each 24 × 24″. Collection Irwin R. Miller, Columbus, Ind.

167

169. *Inflexion.* 1967. Acrylic on canvas, 60 × 60″. Collection the artist

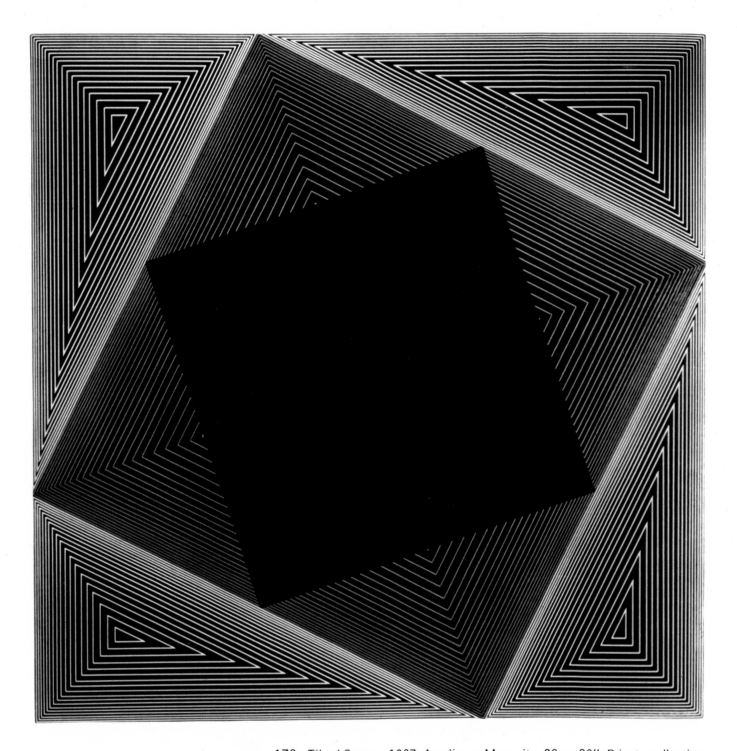

170. *Tilted Square.* 1967. Acrylic on Masonite, 36 × 36″. Private collection

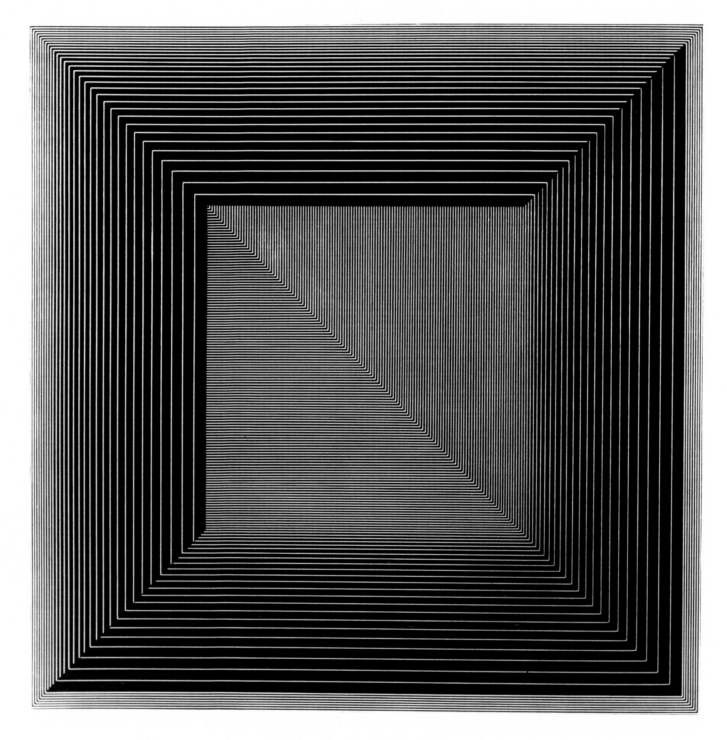

171. *Arithmetical Red.* 1967. Acrylic on Masonite, 36 × 36″. Collection Mr. and Mrs. Lee Schooler

172. *Aureole II: Three-unit Dimensional.* 1967. Enamel on plywood, each square 24″. Collection the artist

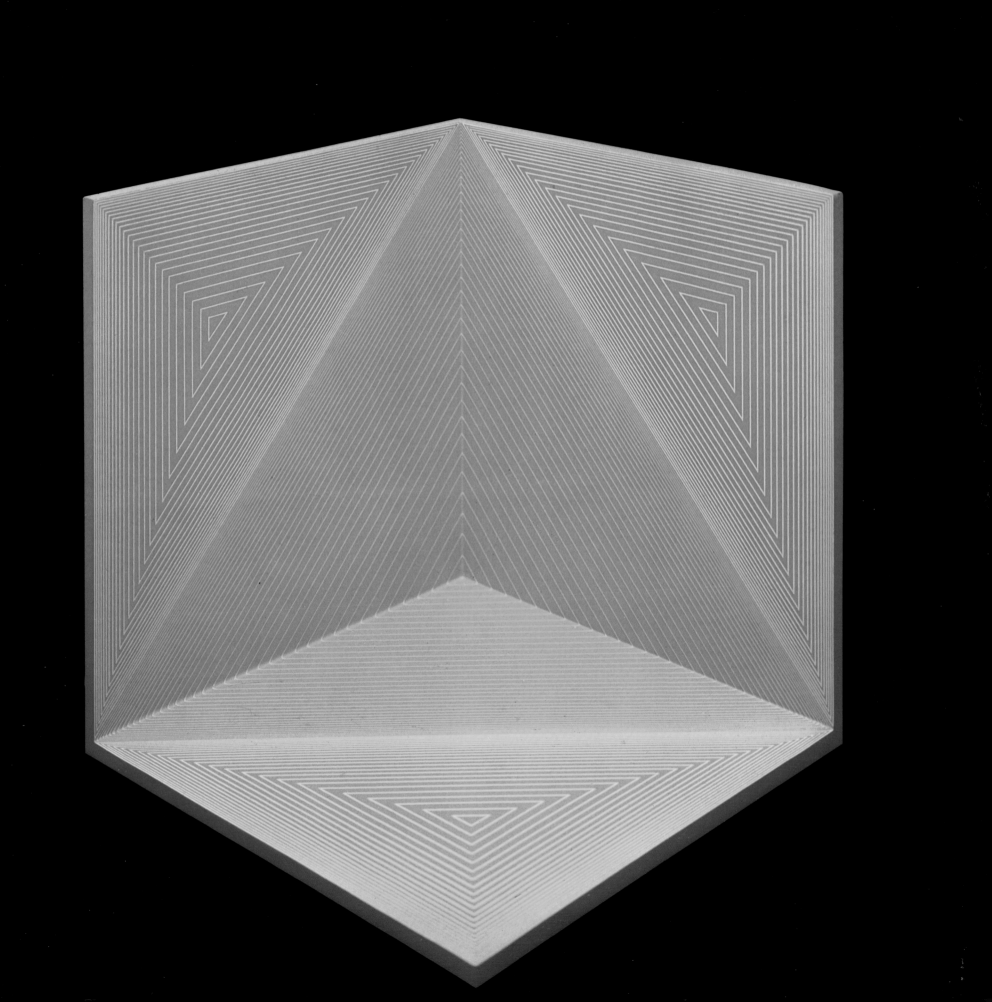

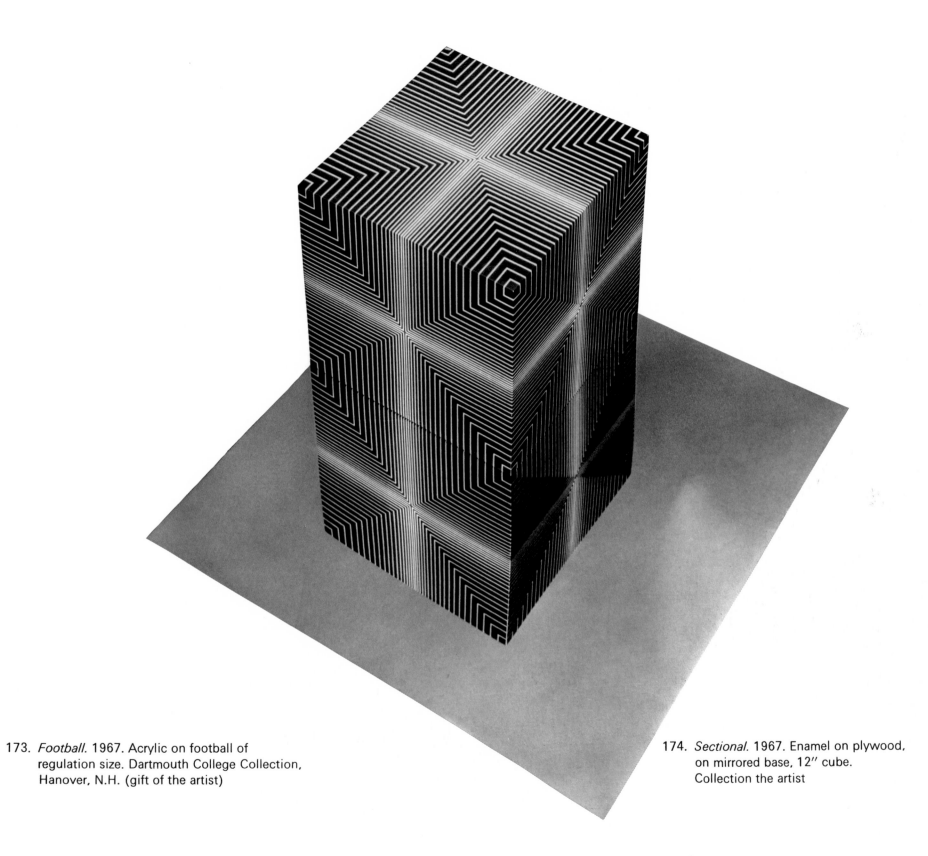

173. *Football.* 1967. Acrylic on football of
regulation size. Dartmouth College Collection,
Hanover, N.H. (gift of the artist)

174. *Sectional.* 1967. Enamel on plywood,
on mirrored base, 12″ cube.
Collection the artist

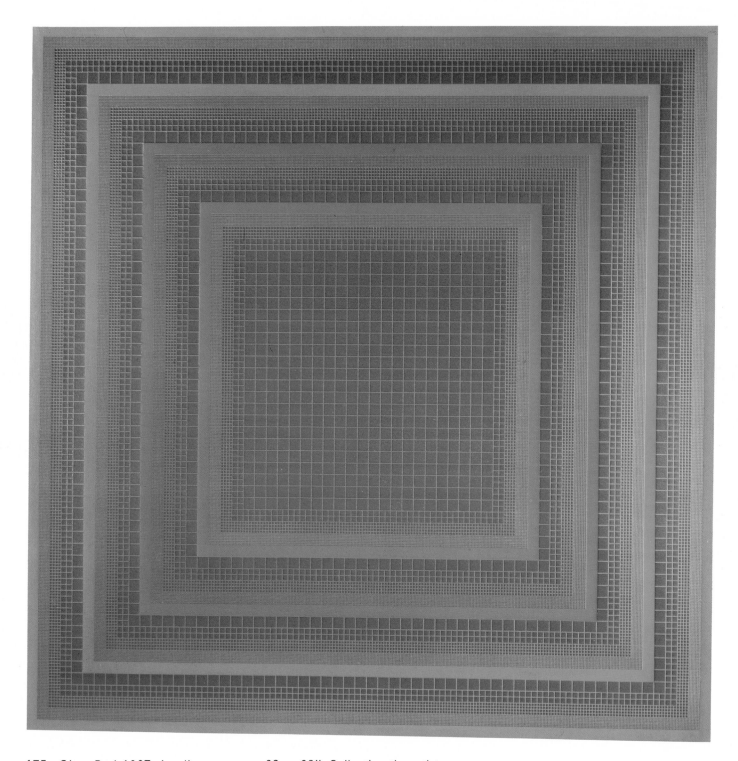

175. *Glory Red.* 1967. Acrylic on canvas, 60 × 60″. Collection the artist

176. *Glory Red.* Detail of plate 175.

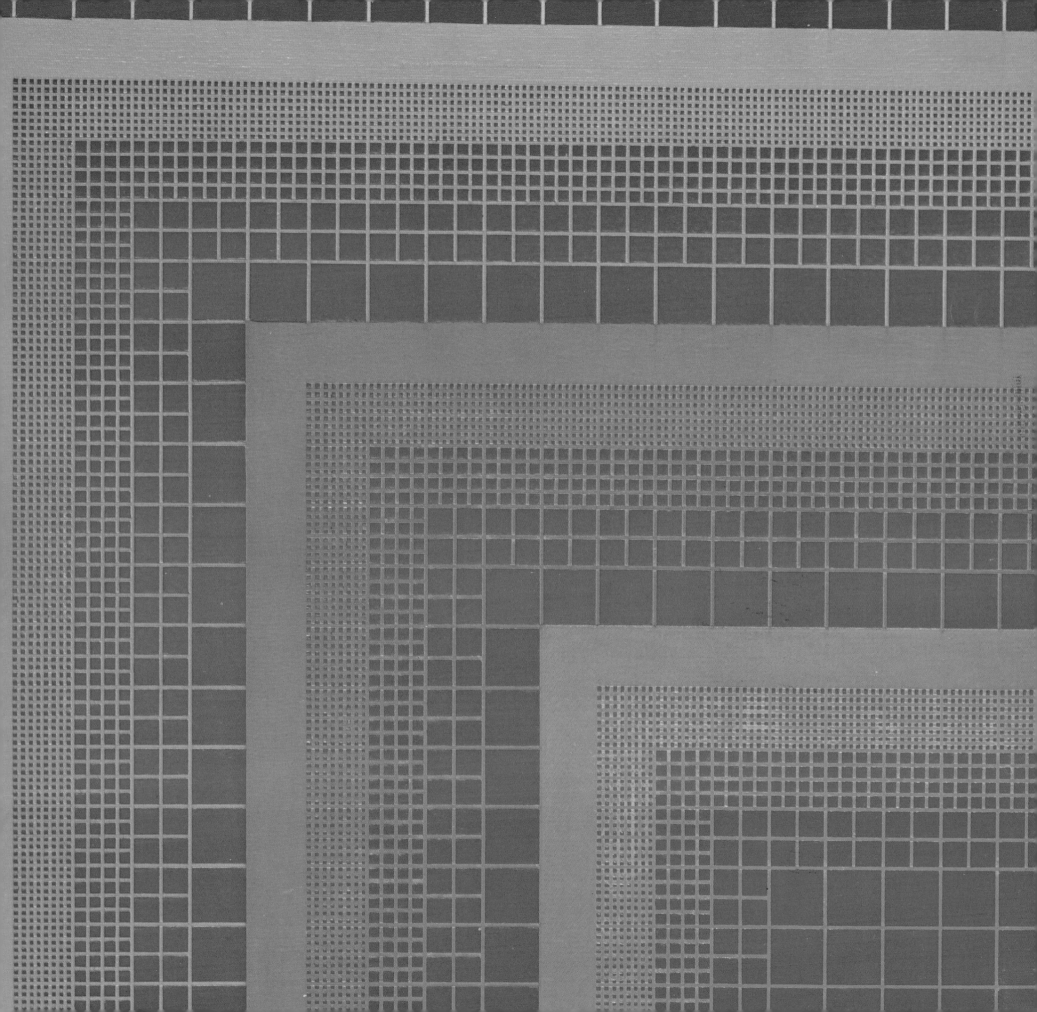

177. *Rectilinear*. 1967. Acrylic on canvas, 60 × 60″. Collection *The Des Moines Register and Tribune*

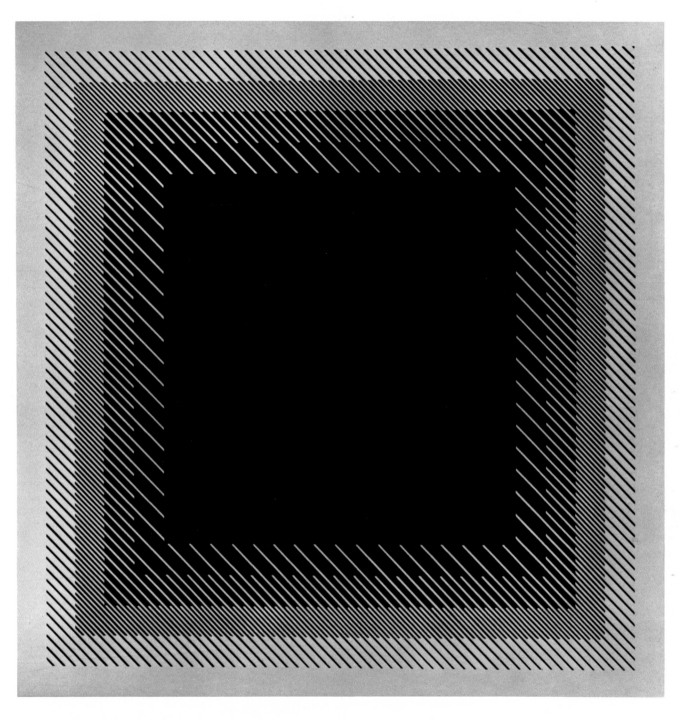

178. *Black and White Series*. 1968. Oil on board, 24 × 24″. American Federation
   of Arts Exhibition (Museum Purchase Fund Collection)

181. *Structured.* 1968. Acrylic on Masonite, 17 × 17″. Private collection

182. *Spectral Cadmium.* 1968. Acrylic on Masonite, 36 × 36″. Private collection

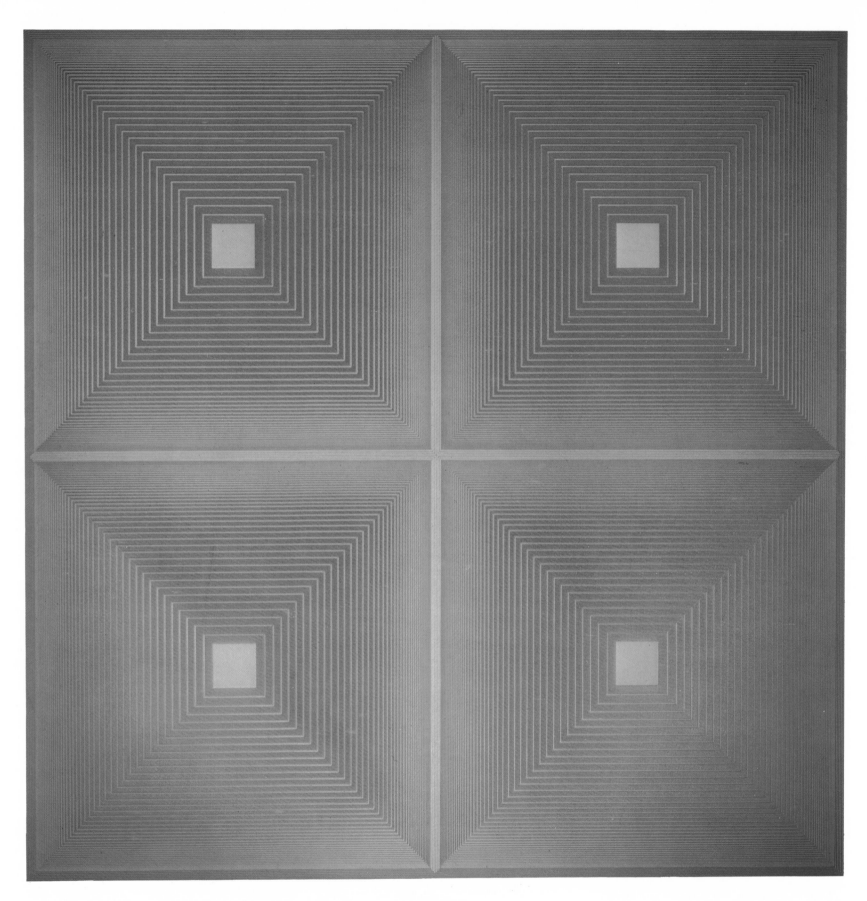

183. *Heat*. 1968. Acrylic on canvas, 84 × 84″. Virginia Museum of Fine Arts, Richmond

184. *Bouquet*. 1968. Acrylic on canvas, 36 × 36″. Collection Mrs. Henry R. Luce, New York

185. *To Josef Albers, II*. 1968. Acrylic on Masonite, 19 × 19″. Private collection

186. *The Blues*. 1969. Acrylic on canvas, 36 × 48″. Collection the artist

187. *Sun Garden*. 1968. Acrylic on canvas, 96 × 96″. Collection Chase Manhattan Bank, New York

188. *Bleached Orange.* 1968. Acrylic on canvas, 48 × 48″. Collection the artist

189. *One Hundred and Twenty-one Squares.* 1969. Acrylic
on canvas, 60 × 60". Private collection

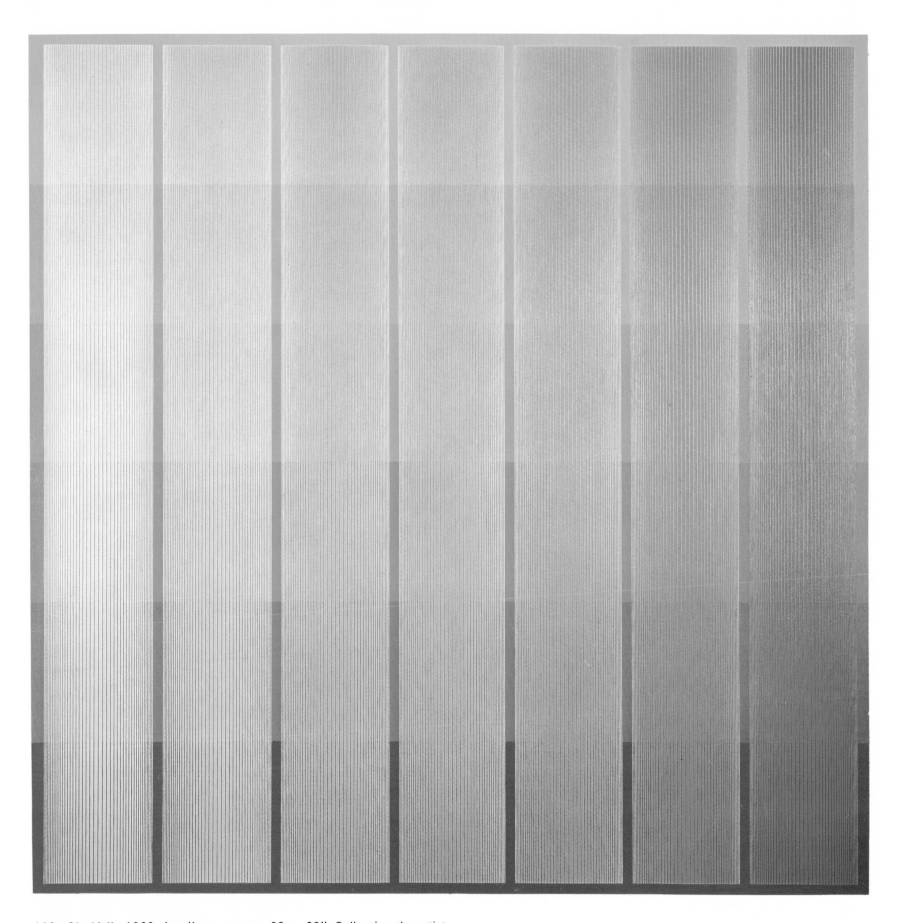

190. *Sky Veils*. 1969. Acrylic on canvas, 60 × 60″. Collection the artist

191. *Neon Game.* 1969. Acrylic on canvas, 60 × 60″. Collection the artist

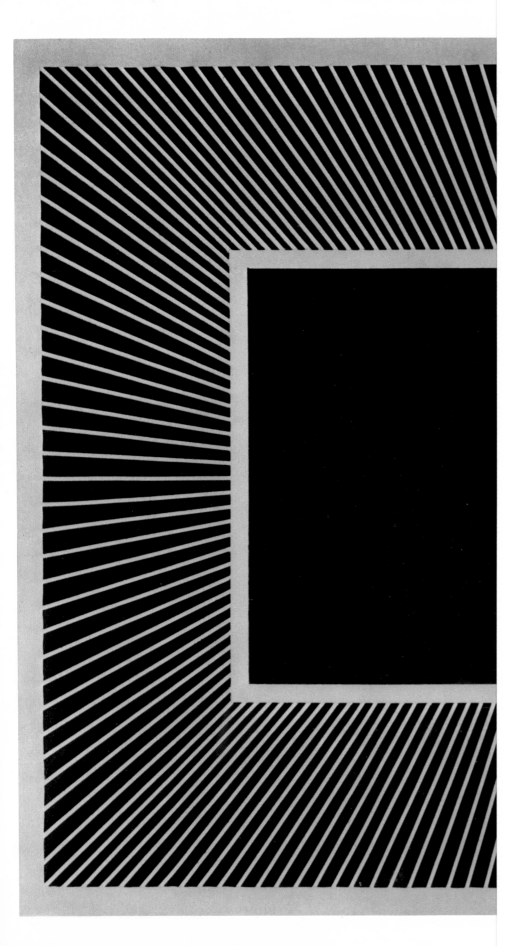

193. *Rosafication*. 1970. Acrylic on canvas,
60 × 60″. Collection the artist

192. *The Union of Mercury and Sulphur*. n.d. Acrylic on
board, 24 × 36″. Collection
Lucille Niebur, New York

194. *Entrance to Green.* 1970. Acrylic on canvas, 108 × 72″. Collection the artist

195. *Sun Game.* 1970. Acrylic on canvas, 60 × 60″. Collection the artist

196. *Trinity*. 1970. Acrylic on canvas, 42 × 72″. Alcoa Collection of Contemporary Art, Pittsburgh

197. *Triangular.* 1970. Acrylic on canvas, 60 × 60". Collection the artist

198. *Tribal*. 1970. Acrylic on canvas, 84 × 84″. Collection Mr. and Mrs. David Teiger, West Orange, N.J.

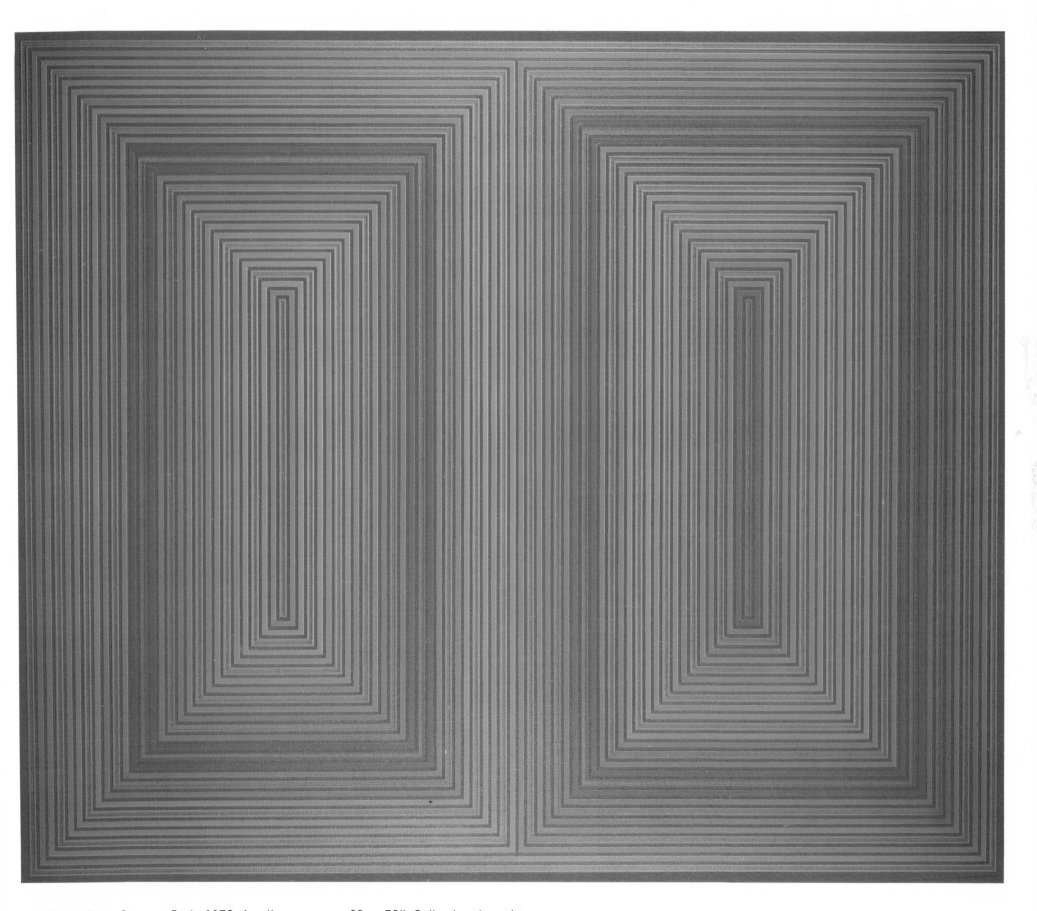

199. *Winter-Summer Reds.* 1973, Acrylic on canvas, 60 × 73″. Collection the artist

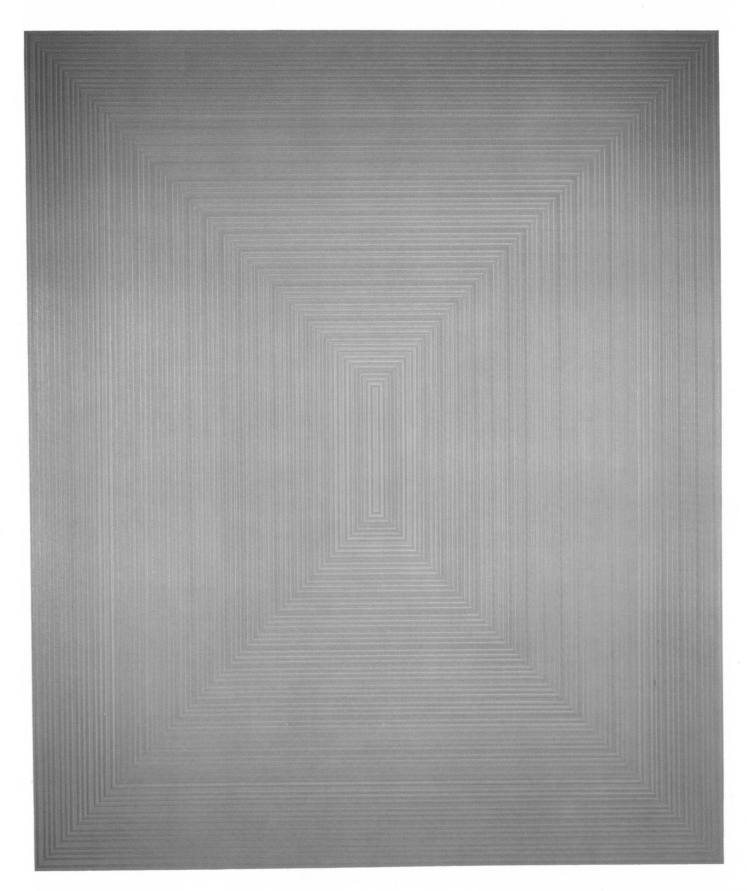

200. *Spring-Warm.* 1973. Acrylic on canvas, 72 × 84″. Collection the artist

BIOGRAPHICAL OUTLINE

1930
May 23, born in Erie, Pennsylvania

1948–53
Attended Cleveland Institute of Art, Ohio. Received Bachelor of Fine Arts degree

1953
Awarded Pulitzer Traveling Scholarship by the National Academy of Design

1953–55
Attended Yale University School of Art and Architecture, New Haven. Studied with Josef Albers. Received Master of Fine Arts degree

1955–56
Attended Kent State University, Kent, Ohio. Received Bachelor of Science degree in education

1957
Moved to New York City

1958
Traveled and studied in Europe and North Africa

1960
Married Elizabeth Feeney

1963–65
Taught at Cooper Union, New York

1967
Artist in Residence, Dartmouth College, Hanover, New Hampshire
Settled in Englewood, New Jersey, where he now lives and maintains his studio

1968
Visiting Artist at University of Wisconsin, Cornell University, and Kent State University

ONE-MAN EXHIBITIONS

1955
The Butler Institute of American Art, Youngstown, Ohio

1960
The Contemporaries, New York

1961
The Contemporaries, New York

1963
The Contemporaries, New York

1965
Sidney Janis Gallery, New York

1966
The Cleveland Museum of Art, Ohio

1967
Sidney Janis Gallery, New York

1968
Kent State University, Kent, Ohio

1969
Sidney Janis Gallery, New York

1971
Sidney Janis Gallery, New York

1972
De Cordova Museum, Lincoln, Massachusetts

Jacksonville Art Museum, Jacksonville, Florida

Loch Haven Art Center, Orlando, Florida

1973
Sidney Janis Gallery, New York

Summit Art Center, Summit, New Jersey

1974–76
United States Information Service traveling exhibition circulated to American embassies in about ten foreign capitals

1975
Andrew Crispo Gallery, New York

1976
Ulrich Museum of Art, Wichita State University, Wichita, Kansas

La Jolla Museum of Contemporary Art, La Jolla, California

Fairlawn Public Library, Fairlawn, New Jersey

1977
Berkeley Museum of Art, Berkeley, California

Columbus Museum of Art, Columbus, Ohio

GROUP EXHIBITIONS

1961

Contemporary American Painting and Sculpture, Krannert Art Museum, University of Illinois, Urbana

First Annual Invitational Art Competition, New York University, New York City

Painting and Sculpture Acquisitions, January 1, 1960—December 31, 1960, The Museum of Modern Art, New York

1962

Contemporary Artists Represented by The Contemporaries Gallery, New York, Tweed Gallery, University of Minnesota, Minneapolis

Geometric Abstraction in America, The Whitney Museum of American Art, New York (shown also in Boston; St. Louis; Columbus, Ohio; and Utica, New York)

Pennsylvania Academy of Design Annual, Philadelphia

Recent American Painting and Sculpture, Atheneum School, Helsinki, Finland

Thirteenth Annual New England Exhibition, Silvermine Guild of Artists, New Canaan, Connecticut

1963

Americans, 1963, The Museum of Modern Art, New York

Annual Exhibition, 1963, The Whitney Museum of American Art, New York

Eleventh Exhibition of Contemporary American Painting and Sculpture, Krannert Art Museum, University of Illinois, Urbana

The Formalists, The Washington Gallery of Modern Art, Washington, D.C.

Fourteenth New England Exhibit of Painting and Sculpture, Silvermine Guild of Artists, New Canaan, Connecticut

The James A. Michener Foundation Collection, Allentown Art Museum, Pennsylvania

New Directions in American Painting, Brandeis University, Waltham, Massachusetts

New Experiments in Art, De Cordova Museum, Lincoln, Massachusetts

1964

American Art Today, Pavilion of Fine Arts, New York World's Fair

The Classic Spirit in Twentieth-century Art, Sidney Janis Gallery, New York

Modern American Drawings, FAR Gallery, New York

Mouvement 2, Galerie Denise René, Paris

The New Formalists, The University of Michigan Museum of Art, Ann Arbor

The 1964 Pittsburgh International Exhibition of Contemporary Painting and Sculpture, Museum of Art, Carnegie Institute, Pittsburgh

Old Hundred: Selections from the Larry Aldrich Contemporary Collection, 1951–1964, The Larry Aldrich Museum of Contemporary Art, Ridgefield, Connecticut

Painting and Sculpture of a Decade, 1954–1964, The Tate Gallery, London

The Silvermine Guild of Artists Fifteenth Annual New England Exhibition, New Canaan, Connecticut. Received painting award

Sixty-seventh Annual Exhibition, The Art Institute of Chicago

1965

Abstract Trompe l'Oeil, Sidney Janis Gallery, New York

Art et Mouvement—Art Optique et Cinétique (in collaboration with Galerie Denise René, Paris), Museum of Tel Aviv, Israel

Art in Process, Finch College Museum of Art, New York

The Bruno Collection, Finch College Museum of Art, New York

Contemporary Art—Acquisitions 1962–1965, The Albright-Knox Art Gallery, Buffalo, New York

The Corcoran Biennial, The Corcoran Gallery of Art, Washington, D.C.

A Decade of American Drawings, 1955–1965, The Whitney Museum of American Art, New York

Kinetic and Optic Art Today, The Albright-Knox Art Gallery, Buffalo, New York

Midyear Show, The Butler Institute of American Art, Youngstown, Ohio

$1 + 1 = 3$: An Exhibition of Retinal and Perceptual Art, University Art Museum, University of Texas, Austin

Pop and Op, an Exhibition of 65 Graphic Works, The American Federation of Arts, New York

The Responsive Eye, The Museum of Modern Art, New York

Seven Americans, The Arkansas Art Center, Little Rock

Vibrations Eleven, Martha Jackson Gallery, New York

1966

Art of the United States, 1670–1966, The Whitney Museum of American Art, New York

The W. Hawkins Ferry Collection, The Detroit Institute of Arts

The First Flint International, Flint Institute of Arts, Michigan

Five Years: The Friends of the Corcoran, The Corcoran Gallery of Art, Washington, D.C.

Radius 5, Lafayette College, Easton, Pennsylvania

Seven Decades, 1895–1965, Cordier and Eckstrom Gallery, New York

Three Generations: Albers, Vasarely, Anuszkiewicz, The J. L. Hudson Gallery, Detroit

The White House Festival of the Arts, Washington, D.C.

1967
American Painting Now, United States Pavilion at Expo '67, Montreal, Canada (also shown at Institute of Contemporary Art, Boston)

The Benjamin Collection, a Loan Exhibition, Yale University Art Gallery, New Haven, Connecticut

Color Image and Form, The Detroit Institute of Arts

Focus on Light, The New Jersey State Museum, Trenton

Galerie der Spiegel, Cologne, West Germany

Geometric Art, The New Jersey State Museum, Trenton

1967 Annual Exhibition of Contemporary American Painting, The Whitney Museum of American Art, New York

The 1967 Pittsburgh International Exhibition of Contemporary Painting and Sculpture, Carnegie Institute, Pittsburgh

Selections from the Collection of Susan Morse Hilles, The Larry Aldrich Museum of Contemporary Art, Ridgefield, Connecticut

1968
The Bradley Collection, Milwaukee Art Center, Wisconsin

Dokumenta IV, Kassel, West Germany

Highlights of the 1967–1968 Art Season, The Larry Aldrich Museum of Contemporary Art, Ridgefield, Connecticut

Icon/Idea, Lafayette College, Easton, Pennsylvania

Paintings from The Albright-Knox Art Gallery, Buffalo, New York, The National Gallery of Art, Washington, D.C.

Plus by Minus, The Albright-Knox Art Gallery, Buffalo, New York

Signals in the 'Sixties, Honolulu Academy of Arts, Hawaii

The Square in Painting, The American Federation of Fine Arts, New York

1969
Contemporary Art—Acquisitions 1966–1969, The Albright-Knox Art Gallery, Buffalo, New York

Exposition–Position, Galerie Denise René, Paris

1969 Annual Exhibition, The Whitney Museum of American Art, New York

Prints and Posters from the U.S.A., U.S. Cultural Center, Tel Aviv, Israel

Sixteenth National Print Exhibition, The Brooklyn Museum, New York

1970
Contemporary American Art, 1870–1970 Centennial Exhibition, Indiana State University, Bloomington

How a Screen Print Is Made, The American Federation of Fine Arts, New York

The 1970 Pittsburgh International Exhibition of Contemporary Painting and Sculpture, Carnegie Institute, Pittsburgh

The Protean Century, 1870–1970, a Loan Exhibition from the Dartmouth College Collection, M. Knoedler, Inc., New York

1971
Anuszkiewicz—Fangor—Segal, Newark State College, Union, New Jersey

Anuszkiewicz—Segal, The New Jersey State College, Trenton

Highlights of the 1970–71 Art Season, The Larry Aldrich Museum of Contemporary Art, Ridgefield, Connecticut

Seventh Triennial—New Jersey Artists, Newark Museum, Newark, New Jersey

The Structure of Color, The Whitney Museum of American Art, New York

Works on Paper, The Art Institute of Chicago

1972
Color Painting, Mead Art Building, Amherst College, Amherst, Massachusetts

Friends of the Delaware Art Museum, Wilmington

Hall Gallery, Miami Beach, Florida

1972 Annual Exhibition, The Whitney Museum of American Art, New York

Recent Paintings and Sculpture, Munson-Williams-Proctor Institute, Utica, New York

1973
Anuszkiewicz—Stanczac, Mansfield Art Center, Mansfield, Ohio

1974
Dealer's Choice, The New York Cultural Center, New York

Opening Exhibition, Hirshhorn Museum and Sculpture Garden, Washington, D.C.

Twentieth-century American Painters, Andrew Crispo Gallery, New York

Twenty-fifth Anniversary Exhibition, Part II, Sidney Janis Gallery, New York

1975
Thirty-fourth Biennial of Contemporary American painting, The Corcoran Gallery of Art, Washington, D.C.

Pittsburgh Corporations Collect, Heinz Galleries, Carnegie Institute, Pittsburgh, Pennsylvania

The Growing Spectrum of American Art, Joslyn Art Museum, Omaha, Nebraska

Forms of Color, Akron Art Institute, Akron, Ohio

1976
Painting and Sculpture Today, Indianapolis Museum of Art, Indianapolis, Indiana

BIBLIOGRAPHY

BOOKS

Albers, Josef. *Interaction of Color* (rev. ed.). New Haven, Conn., and London: Yale University Press, 1975

Alloway, Lawrence. "Notes on Op Art." In *The New Art: A Critical Anthology* (Gregory Battcock, ed.), pp. 83–91. New York: E. P. Dutton & Co., 1966

Anuszkiewicz, Richard. "A Study in the Creation of Space with Life Drawing." M.F.A. thesis, Yale University, 1955

Arnason, H. H. *History of Modern Art: Painting, Sculpture, Architecture.* New York: Harry N. Abrams, [1968]

Arnheim, Rudolf. *Art and Visual Perception: A Psychology of the Creative Eye* (exp. and rev. ed.). Berkeley and Los Angeles: University of California Press, 1974

———— *Toward a Psychology of Art: Collected Essays.* Berkeley and Los Angeles: University of California Press, 1966

———— *Visual Thinking.* Berkeley and Los Angeles: University of California Press, 1969

Barrett, Cyril. *Op Art.* New York: The Viking Press, 1970

Birren, Faber. *History of Color in Painting: With New Principles of Color Expression.* New York: Reinhold Publishing Corporation, 1965

Boring, Edwin G. *Sensation and Perception in the History of Experimental Psychology.* New York: Appleton-Century-Crofts, 1942

Chevreul, Michel Eugène. *The Principles of Harmony and Contrast of Colors and Their Application to the Arts* (repr.). New York and London: Reinhold Publishing Corporation, 1967

Elsen, Albert E. *Purposes of Art: An Introduction to the History and Appreciation of Art* (2d ed.). New York and London: Holt, Rinehart and Winston, n.d. [1967]

Encyclopaedia Britannica, vol. I, p. 434. Chicago: Encyclopaedia Britannica, Inc., 1974

Encyclopedia of World Art, vol. X, cols. 204, 769. New York: McGraw-Hill, 1965

Fuller, R. Buckminster, and Robert Marks. *The Dymaxion World of Buckminster Fuller* (rev. ed.). Garden City, N.Y.: Anchor Books/Doubleday, 1973

Gibson, Eleanor J. *Principles of Perceptual Learning and Development.* New York: Appleton-Century-Crofts, 1969

Gibson, James J. *The Perception of the Visual World.* Boston and San Francisco: Houghton Mifflin Company, The Riverside Press, 1950

———— *The Senses Considered as Perceptual Systems.* Boston: Houghton Mifflin Company, 1966

Hunter, Sam. *La pittura americana del dopoguerra.* Milan: Fratelli Fabbri, 1970

———— and John Jacobus. *American Art of the Twentieth Century: Painting, Sculpture, Architecture.* New York: Harry N. Abrams, [1973]

Itten, Johannes. *The Art of Color: The Subjective Experience and Objective Rationale of Color* (Ernst van Haagen, trans.). New York and Melbourne: Van Nostrand Reinhold Company, 1961

Ivins, William M., Jr. *Art & Geometry: A Study in Space Intuitions.* Cambridge, Mass.: Harvard University Press, 1946; New York: Dover Publications, 1964 (repr.)

Knobler, Nathan. *The Visual Dialogue:*

An Introduction to the Appreciation of Art (2d ed.). New York: Holt, Rinehart and Winston, 1971

Koffka, K[urt]. *Principles of Gestalt Psychology.* New York: Harcourt, Brace and Company, 1935; A Harbinger Book (paperback), 1963

Luckiesh, M. *Visual Illusions: Their Causes, Characteristics and Applications* (new introd. by William H. Ittleson). New York: Dover Publications, 1965

Mellow, James A. "Art Explosion." In *The New York Times Encyclopedic Almanac 1970* (Seymour Kurz, ed.), pp. 629–30. New York: World Publishing Co., 1969

Mendelowitz, Daniel M. *A History of American Art* (2d ed.). New York: Holt, Rinehart and Winston, 1970

Ostwald, Wilhelm. *The Color Primer: A Basic Treatise on the Color System of Wilhelm Ostwald* (foreword and evaluation by Faber Birren, ed.). New York and Melbourne: Van Nostrand Reinhold Company, 1969 [original German ed., 1916]

Parola, Rene. *Optical Art: Theory and Practice.* New York and Amsterdam: Reinhold Book Corporation, 1969

Popper, Frank. *Origins and Development of Kinetic Art* (Stephen Bann, trans.). Greenwich, Conn.: New York Graphic Society, n.d.; London: Studio Vista, 1968

Rickey, George. *Constructivism: Origins and Evolution.* New York: George Braziller, 1967

Rood, Ogden N. *Modern Chromatics: Students' Text-Book of Color with Applications to Art and Industry* (including a facsimile of the first American ed. [New York: D. Appleton and Company, 1879]; preface, introduction and commentary notes by Faber Birren). New York and Melbourne: Van Nostrand Reinhold Company, 1973

Woody, Russell O., Jr. *Polymer Painting, and Related Techniques*. New York and Melbourne: Van Nostrand Reinhold Company, n.d.

PERIODICALS

Amaya, Mario. "Trays by Ten Artists," *Art in America*, vol. 59, January/February, 1971, pp. 48–57

Arnason, H. H. "The Precisionists: The New Geometry," *Art in America*, vol. 48, no. 3, 1960, pp. 54–61

Baro, Gene. "New York Exhibitions: A Gathering of Americans," *Arts Magazine*, vol. 37, September, 1963, pp. 28–33

B[enediki], M[ichael]. "Reviews and Previews," *Art News*, vol. 69, no. 10, February, 1971, p. 17

Bowness, Alan. "54/64 Painting and Sculpture of a Decade: The Gulbenkian Exhibition," *Studio International*, vol. 167, May 1964, pp. 190–95

B[uehr], W[endy]. "A Banner Year for Banners," *Horizon*, vol. 6, Spring 1964, pp. 60–65.

B[urrows], C[arlyle]. "Art Exhibition Notes: 'Scientific' Designs," *New York Herald Tribune*, Apr. 8, 1961, p. 5

Canaday, John. "American Drawings: Or, the Sad Case of the Hidden Virtues," *The New York Times*, Oct. 25, 1964, sec. 2, p. 13

——— "Americans Once More," *The New York Times*, May 26, 1963, sec. 2, p. 11

——— "Art: Eakins in New York at Last," *The New York Times*, Sept. 27, 1970, sec. 2, p. 23

——— "Art: Fifteen Exhibit at Modern," *The New York Times*, May 22, 1963, p. 38

——— "Art: Optics Are the Stalk of the Town," *The New York Times*, Jan. 30, 1965, p. 24

——— "Art That Pulses, Quivers and Fascinates," *The New York Times Magazine*, Feb. 21, 1965, pp. 12–13, 55–57, 59

——— "The Responsive Eye: Three Cheers and High Hopes," Feb. 28, 1965, sec. 2, p. 19

——— "Richard Anuszkiewicz: It's Baffling," *The New York Times*, Apr. 5, 1969, p. 23

Chapin, Louis. "New York Reviews," *Art News*, vol. 74, no. 5, May, 1975, pp. 98–99

Coates, Robert M. "The Art Galleries: 'Op'," *The New Yorker*, vol. 41, Mar. 27, 1965, pp. 161–64, 167

Doty, Robert. "Richard Anuszkiewicz," *Museum News*, vol. 48, January, 1970, pp. 11–12

Eye: Magazine of the Yale Arts Association, no. 2, 1968

Genauer, Emily. "138 Pictures by Living Artists: American Art Survey: '65 Edition at Whitney," *New York Herald Tribune*, Dec. 8, 1965, p. 29

——— "The Wizards of Op," *New York: The Sunday Herald Tribune Magazine*, Feb. 21, 1965, pp. 30, 32, 58

Getlein, Frank. "Biennial Show at the Corcoran," *Washington Sunday Star*, Feb. 28, 1965

Glueck, Grace. "Art Notes: Blues and Greens on Reds," *The New York Times*, Feb. 21, 1965, sec. 2, p. 19

——— "Out of St. Cyr: Furrier to the Art World," *The New York Times Magazine*, Oct. 2, 1966, pp. 39, 135–39

Gray, Cleve. "Ceramics by Twelve Artists," *Art in America*, vol. 52, December, 1964, pp. 27–41

Gruen, John. "Art: 'Op' Pops and Their Opsprings," *New York: The Sunday Herald Tribune Magazine*, Feb. 7, 1965, p. 32.

——— "Pop Goes the Easel," *New York Herald Tribune*, May 26, 1963, sec. 4, p. 6

Jacobs, Jay. "Pertinent & Impertinent: Publisher," *TheARTgallery Magazine*, vol. 13, October, 1969

——— "Portrait of the Artist—Richard Anuszkiewicz," *TheARTgallery Magazine*, vol. 14, March, 1971, pp. 21–35

Jameson, Dorothea, and Leo M. Hurvich. "From Contrast to Assimilation: in Art and in the Eye," *Leonardo*, vol 8, 1975, pp. 125–131

Jersey City Awake: A City in Transition (pamphlet), New Jersey State Council on the Arts, Trenton, N.J., n.d. [1972]

Karshan, Donald H. "Graphics '70: Richard Anuszkiewicz," *Art in America*, vol. 58, March/April, 1970, pp. 56–59

Kramer, Hilton. "Art: Clashing Values of Two Generations," *The New York Times*, Nov. 6, 1965, p. 26

Krauss, Rosalind. "Afterthoughts on 'Op'," *Art International*, vol. 9, June, 1965, pp. 75–76

K[urtz], S[tephen] A. "Reviews and Previews," *Art News*, vol. 68, no. 2, April, 1969, p. 8

Lunde, Karl. "Richard Anuszkiewicz," *Arts Magazine*, February, 1975, pp. 56–57

Lynes, Russell. "The Mesh Canvas," *Art in America*, vol. 56, May/June, 1968, pp. 28–49

Mayor, A. Hyatt. "Painters' Playing Cards," *Art in America*, vol. 51, no. 2, 1963, pp. 39–42

Milwaukee Art Center Annual Report 1969, May, 1970

Morris, Bernardine. "Anuszkiewicz Sets Legs into Motion," *The New York Times*, May 29, 1965, p. 15

Neumann, Eckhard. "Op-Art," *Kunst*, vol. 5, February/April, 1965, pp. 36–41

"O Say Can You See," *Newsweek*, vol. 65, Jan. 11, 1965, p. 78

O'Doherty, Brian. "Art: 'The Classic Spirit'," *The New York Times*, Feb. 4, 1964, p. 66

"Op: Adventure Without Danger," *Newsweek*, vol. 65, Mar. 1, 1965, pp. 82–83

"Op Art: Pictures That Attack the Eye," *Time*, vol. 84, Oct. 23, 1964, pp. 78–86

Ortman, George. "Artists' Games," *Art in America*, vol. 57, November/December, 1969, pp. 69–77

"Painting and Sculpture Acquisitions, 1960," *The Museum of Modern Art Bulletin*, vol. 28, nos. 2–4, pp. 5, 54–55

P[erreault], J[ohn]. "Reviews and Previews," *Art News*, vol. 66, no. 6, October, 1967, p. 12

Preston, Stuart. "Adventures and Renewals: Slight of Eye," *The New York Times*, Apr. 2, 1961, sec. 2, p. 16

———— "'Les Animaliers' Stage Comeback," *The New York Times*, Mar. 4, 1963, p. 9

———— "Art: American Geometric Abstraction," *The New York Times*, Mar. 21, 1962, p. 36

———— "Connecticut Sets the Pace," *The New York Times*, July 5, 1964, sec. 2, p. 15

"Recent Acquisition," *Virginia Museum Bulletin*, vol. 31, September, 1970, n.p.

"Recent Acquisitions," *City Art Museum of Saint Louis Bulletin*, vol. 2, May/June, 1966, cover and pp. 1–3

"Richard Anuszkiewicz: Primary Contrast," *Currier Gallery of Art Bulletin*, July/August, 1966

Rickey, George. "Scandale de Succès," *Art International*, vol. 9, May, 1965, pp. 16–23

Roditi, Edouard. "International Reports: Paris: A Theology of Hard-Edge," *Arts Magazine*, vol. 38, December, 1963, pp. 34–37

Rose, Barbara. "New York Letter," *Art International*, vol. 7, Apr. 25, 1963, pp. 57–60

Rosenberg, Harold. "The Art Galleries: Black and Pistachio," *The New Yorker*, vol. 39, June 15, 1964, p. 84 ff.

———— "From Pollock to Pop: Twenty Years of Painting and Sculpture," *Holiday*, vol. 39, March, 1966, pp. 96–105, 136–38, 140

Rosenthal, Nan. "Brightening the Scene —List Art Posters," *Art in America*, vol. 53, April, 1965, pp. 56–65

Russell, John. "Collector: Larry Aldrich," *Art in America*, vol. 57, January/February, 1969, pp. 56–65

Seitz, William C. "The New Perceptual Art," *Vogue*, vol. 145, Feb. 15, 1965, pp. 78–80, 142–43

Sheppard, Eugenia. "Inside Fashion: Pop Furs May Be Popular," *New York Herald Tribune*, June 9, 1963, sec. 1, p. 28

Shirey, David L. "Reviews and Previews," *Art News*, vol. 72, no. 2, February, 1973, pp. 82–83

"Simple Form, Simple Color," *Time*, vol. 82, July 19, 1963, pp. 56–57, 59

Slate, Joseph. "So Hard to Look at: An Interview with Richard Anuszkiewicz," *Contempora*, May/June, 1970

Smith, Miles A. "Pop Art Losing Its Shock Appeal?" *Daily American*, July 4, 1963

Taylor, Brie. "Towards a Plastic Revolution," *Art News*, vol. 63, March, 1964, pp. 46–49, 62–63

Tillim, Sidney. "Optical Art: Pending or Ending?" *Arts Magazine*, vol. 39, January, 1965, pp. 16–23

Todd, Anne G. "'Op' Show Is Fascinating," *Seattle Times*, July 18, 1965

Willard, Charlotte. "Alfred Barr: New York Forecaster of Trends in Modern Art," *Look*, vol. 27, Mar. 26, 1963, pp. 86–88

———— "Art Centers: New York: Dealers-Eye View," *Art in America*, vol. 52, April, 1964, p. 120 ff.

———— "Drawing Today," *Art in America*, vol. 52, October, 1964, pp. 49–67

EXHIBITION CATALOGUES

Albright-Knox Art Gallery, Buffalo, N.Y. *Art Today: Kinetic and Optic*, 1965

———— *Contemporary Art—Acquisitions 1962–1965*, 1965

———— *Contemporary Art—Acquisitions 1966–1969*, 1969

———— *Plus by Minus: Today's Half-Century* (text by Douglas MacAgy), 1968

The American Federation of Arts, New York. *How a Screen Print Is Made* (introd. by H. L. C. Jaffe; text by Eric Vietze), 1970

———— *Pop and Op* (foreword by George Weissman; introd. by Max Kozloff; sponsored by Philip Morris, Inc.), n.p., [1965 ?]

———— *The Square in Painting* (selected by Richard Anuszkiewicz), 1969

Andrew Crispo Gallery, New York. *Rich-*

ard Anuszkiewicz: Recent Paintings, 1975

The Arkansas Arts Center, Little Rock. Seven Americans, 1965

The Art Institute of Chicago. Sixty-seventh Annual American Exhibition: Directions in American Painting, 1964

Brandeis University, Poses Institute of Fine Arts, Waltham, Mass. New Directions in American Painting, 1963

The Brooklyn Museum, Brooklyn, N.Y. Sixteenth National Print Exhibition: Two Decades of American Prints 1947–1968 (introd. by Una E. Johnson), 1968

The Butler Institute of American Art, Youngstown, Ohio. Thirtieth Annual Midyear Show, [1965]

Carnegie Institute Museum of Art, Pittsburgh, Penn. The 1964 Pittsburgh International: Exhibition of Contemporary Painting and Sculpture (foreword by Gustave von Groschwitz), 1964

————— The 1967 Pittsburgh International Exhibition of Contemporary Painting and Sculpture (foreword by Gustave von Groschwitz), 1967

————— The 1970 Pittsburgh International Exhibition of Contemporary Art (introd. by Leon Anthony Arkus), 1970

The Corcoran Gallery of Art, Washington, D.C. Five Years: The Friends of the Corcoran, "The Contemporary Spirit" (preface by Hermann Warner Williams, Jr.), 1966

————— The Twenty-ninth Biennial Exhibition of Contemporary American Painting (introd. by Hermann Warner Williams, Jr.), 1965

Dartmouth College Arts Council, Dartmouth College, Hanover, N.H. The Protean Century 1870–1970: A Loan Exhibition from The Dartmouth College Collection, Alumni and Friends of the College, 1970

DeCordova Museum, Lincoln, Mass. New Experiments in Art, 1963

————— Paintings by Richard Anuszkiewicz (foreword by Carlo M. Lamagna), 1972

The Detroit Institute of Arts. The W. Hawkins Ferry Collection (introd. by Joshua C. Taylor), 1966

Ferdinand Roten Galleries, Inc., Baltimore, Md. Catalogue No. 12, 1970

Finch College Museum of Art, New York, The Josephine and Phillip A. Bruno Collection, 1965

Flint Institute of Arts, Flint, Mich. The First Flint Invitational: An Exhibition of Contemporary Painting and Sculpture (foreword by G. Stuart Hodge), 1966

Galerie Denise René, Paris. Exposition-Position, 1969

————— Mouvement 2, 1964

Honolulu Academy of Arts. Signals in the 'Sixties (foreword by James W. Foster, Jr.; introd. by James Johnson Sweeney), 1968

Hudson Company, The J. L., Detroit. Three Generations: Albers, Vasarely, Anuszkiewicz, 1966

Illinois, University of, Urbana, College of Fine and Applied Arts, Krannert Art Museum. Contemporary American Painting and Sculpture (foreword by C. V. Donovan; text by Allen S. Weller), University of Illinois Press, 1961

————— Eleventh Exhibition of Contemporary American Painting and Sculpture, 1963 (foreword by C. V. Donovan; introd. by Allen S. Weller), University of Illinois Press, 1963

Indiana State University, Bloomington, Ind., Turman Art Gallery. Contemporary American Art, 1870–1970 Centennial Exhibition, 1970

Institute of Contemporary Art, Boston. American Painting Now (introd. by Alan Solomon), 1967

Kent State University, Kent, Ohio, Van

Deusen Gallery. Fifteen Paintings/Anuszkiewicz, 1968

Lafayette College, Easton, Pa. Icon/Idea: Josef Albers, Richard Anuszkiewicz, Clarence Carter, Paul Jenkins, George Ortman (introd. by James A. Michener), 1968

————— Radius 5 (foreword by James A. Michener), 1966

The Larry Aldrich Museum [of Contemporary Art], Ridgefield, Conn. Art of the 50's and 60's: Selections from the Richard Brown Baker Collection (statements by Larry Aldrich and Richard Brown Baker), 1965

————— Highlights of the 1967–68 Art Season, 1968

————— "Old Hundred," Selections from the Larry Aldrich Contemporary Collection, 1951–1964, 1964

————— Selections from the Collection of Susan Morse Hilles (introd. by Larry Aldrich; statement by Susan Morse Hilles), [1967]

Lyman Allyn Museum, New London, Conn. Selections from the Collection of Susan Morse Hilles (foreword by Edgar deN. Mayhew), [1967]

Martha Jackson Gallery, New York. Vibrations Eleven, 1965

The Metropolitan Museum of Art, New York. New York Painting and Sculpture: 1940–1970 (text by Henry Geldzahler), E. P. Dutton & Co., 1969

Michigan, University of, Ann Arbor, Mich., Museum of Art. The New Formalists. Contemporary American Paintings for Purchase Considerations, 1964

Milwaukee Art Center. The Collection of Mrs. Harry Lynde Bradley (introd. by Tracy Atkinson), 1968

The Museum of Modern Art, New York. Americans 1963 (edited by Dorothy C. Miller, with statements by the artists and others), 1963

————— The Responsive Eye (text by William C. Seitz), 1965

203

——— *The Sidney and Harriet Janis Collection: A Gift to The Museum of Modern Art* (preface by Alfred H. Barr, Jr.), 1968

National Gallery of Art, Washington, D.C. *Paintings from the Albright-Knox Art Gallery, Buffalo, New York* (foreword by John Walker), 1968

The New Jersey State Museum, Trenton, N.J. *Focus on Light* (organized by Richard Bellamy, Lucy R. Lippard, and Leah P. Sloshberg; foreword by Edward A. Ring; essay by Lucy R. Lippard), 1967

——— *Geometric Art: An Exhibition of Paintings and Constructions by Fourteen Contemporary New Jersey Artists* (foreword by Leah Phyfer Sloshberg), 1967

——— *Paintings by Richard Anuszkiewicz/Sculpture by George Segal* (foreword by Leah Sloshberg; introd. by Zoltan Buki), 1971

New York World's Fair, 1964, Pavilion of Fine Arts. *American Art Today* (presented by Long Island Arts Center, Inc.), n.p., n.d.

Public Education Association, New York. *Seven Decades 1895–1965: Cross Currents in Modern Art* (text by Peter Selz), 1966

Sidney Janis Gallery, New York. *Anuszkiewicz,* 1971

——— *Anuszkiewicz: New Paintings,* 1969

——— *New Paintings by Anuszkiewicz,* 1965

——— *New Paintings by Anuszkiewicz,* 1967

——— *Pop and Op,* 1964

Silvermine Guild of Artists, New Canaan, Conn. *Silvermine Guild of Artists Fifteenth Annual New England Exhibition,* 1964

Tel Aviv, Museum of. *Art et mouvement—art optique et cinétique* (organized in collaboration with the Galerie Denise René, Paris), 1965

Tel Aviv, United States Cultural Center. *Prints and Posters from the U.S.A.* (foreword by John D. Congleton), 1969

Texas, The University of, Austin, The University Art Museum. *1 + 1 = 3: An Exhibition of Retinal and Perceptual Art* (introd. by Donald B. Goodall; statement by Vincent Mariani), n.d.

United States Information Service. *Anuszkiewicz,* [Washington, D.C.], 1974

Washington Gallery of Modern Art, Washington, D.C. *The Formalists,* 1963

Whitney Museum of American Art, New York. *Annual Exhibition 1963: Contemporary American Painting,* [1963]

——— *Annual Exhibition 1966: Contemporary Sculpture and Prints,* [1966]

——— *Art of the United States: 1670–1966,* 2 vols. (text by Lloyd Goodrich), 1966

——— *A Decade of American Drawings 1955–1965: Eighth Exhibition Sponsored by the Friends* (foreword by Donald M. Blinken), [1965]

——— *Geometric Abstraction in America: Fifth Loan Exhibition, Friends of the Whitney Museum of American Art* (essay by John Gordon), 1962

——— *1965 Annual Exhibition of Contemporary American Painting,* [1965]

——— *1967 Annual Exhibition of Contemporary Painting,* [1967]

——— *1969 Annual Exhibition, Contemporary American Painting,* [1969]

——— *1972 Annual Exhibition, Contemporary American Painting,* [1972]

——— *The Structure of Color* (text by Marcia Tucker), 1971

Yale University Art Gallery, New Haven, Conn. *The Helen W. and Robert M. Benjamin Collection: A Loan Exhibition* (introd. by Lloyd Goodrich), 1967

BIOGRAPHICAL OUTLINE

1930
May 23, born in Erie, Pennsylvania

1948–53
Attended Cleveland Institute of Art, Ohio. Received Bachelor of Fine Arts degree

1953
Awarded Pulitzer Traveling Scholarship by the National Academy of Design

1953–55
Attended Yale University School of Art and Architecture, New Haven. Studied with Josef Albers. Received Master of Fine Arts degree

1955–56
Attended Kent State University, Kent, Ohio. Received Bachelor of Science degree in education

1957
Moved to New York City

1958
Traveled and studied in Europe and North Africa

1960
Married Elizabeth Feeney

1963–65
Taught at Cooper Union, New York

1967
Artist in Residence, Dartmouth College, Hanover, New Hampshire
Settled in Englewood, New Jersey, where he now lives and maintains his studio

1968
Visiting Artist at University of Wisconsin, Cornell University, and Kent State University

ONE-MAN EXHIBITIONS

1955
The Butler Institute of American Art, Youngstown, Ohio

1960
The Contemporaries, New York

1961
The Contemporaries, New York

1963
The Contemporaries, New York

1965
Sidney Janis Gallery, New York

1966
The Cleveland Museum of Art, Ohio

1967
Sidney Janis Gallery, New York

1968
Kent State University, Kent, Ohio

1969
Sidney Janis Gallery, New York

1971
Sidney Janis Gallery, New York

1972
De Cordova Museum, Lincoln, Massachusetts

Jacksonville Art Museum, Jacksonville, Florida

Loch Haven Art Center, Orlando, Florida

1973
Sidney Janis Gallery, New York

Summit Art Center, Summit, New Jersey

1974–76
United States Information Service traveling exhibition circulated to American embassies in about ten foreign capitals

1975
Andrew Crispo Gallery, New York

1976
Ulrich Museum of Art, Wichita State University, Wichita, Kansas

La Jolla Museum of Contemporary Art, La Jolla, California

Fairlawn Public Library, Fairlawn, New Jersey

1977
Berkeley Museum of Art, Berkeley, California

Columbus Museum of Art, Columbus, Ohio

GROUP EXHIBITIONS

1961
Contemporary American Painting and Sculpture, Krannert Art Museum, University of Illinois, Urbana

First Annual Invitational Art Competition, New York University, New York City

Painting and Sculpture Acquisitions, January 1, 1960—December 31, 1960, The Museum of Modern Art, New York

1962
Contemporary Artists Represented by The Contemporaries Gallery, New York, Tweed Gallery, University of Minnesota, Minneapolis

Geometric Abstraction in America, The Whitney Museum of American Art, New York (shown also in Boston; St. Louis; Columbus, Ohio; and Utica, New York)

Pennsylvania Academy of Design Annual, Philadelphia

Recent American Painting and Sculpture, Atheneum School, Helsinki, Finland

Thirteenth Annual New England Exhibition, Silvermine Guild of Artists, New Canaan, Connecticut

1963
Americans, 1963, The Museum of Modern Art, New York

Annual Exhibition, 1963, The Whitney Museum of American Art, New York

Eleventh Exhibition of Contemporary American Painting and Sculpture, Krannert Art Museum, University of Illinois, Urbana

The Formalists, The Washington Gallery of Modern Art, Washington, D.C.

Fourteenth New England Exhibit of Painting and Sculpture, Silvermine Guild of Artists, New Canaan, Connecticut

The James A. Michener Foundation Collection, Allentown Art Museum, Pennsylvania

New Directions in American Painting, Brandeis University, Waltham, Massachusetts

New Experiments in Art, De Cordova Museum, Lincoln, Massachusetts

1964
American Art Today, Pavilion of Fine Arts, New York World's Fair

The Classic Spirit in Twentieth-century Art, Sidney Janis Gallery, New York

Modern American Drawings, FAR Gallery, New York

Mouvement 2, Galerie Denise René, Paris

The New Formalists, The University of Michigan Museum of Art, Ann Arbor

The 1964 Pittsburgh International Exhibition of Contemporary Painting and Sculpture, Museum of Art, Carnegie Institute, Pittsburgh

Old Hundred: Selections from the Larry Aldrich Contemporary Collection, 1951—1964, The Larry Aldrich Museum of Contemporary Art, Ridgefield, Connecticut

Painting and Sculpture of a Decade, 1954—1964, The Tate Gallery, London

The Silvermine Guild of Artists Fifteenth Annual New England Exhibition, New Canaan, Connecticut. Received painting award

Sixty-seventh Annual Exhibition, The Art Institute of Chicago

1965
Abstract Trompe l'Oeil, Sidney Janis Gallery, New York

Art et Mouvement—Art Optique et Cinétique (in collaboration with Galerie Denise René, Paris), Museum of Tel Aviv, Israel

Art in Process, Finch College Museum of Art, New York

The Bruno Collection, Finch College Museum of Art, New York

Contemporary Art—Acquisitions 1962—1965, The Albright-Knox Art Gallery, Buffalo, New York

The Corcoran Biennial, The Corcoran Gallery of Art, Washington, D.C.

A Decade of American Drawings, 1955—1965, The Whitney Museum of American Art, New York

Kinetic and Optic Art Today, The Albright-Knox Art Gallery, Buffalo, New York

Midyear Show, The Butler Institute of American Art, Youngstown, Ohio

$1 + 1 = 3$: An Exhibition of Retinal and Perceptual Art, University Art Museum, University of Texas, Austin

Pop and Op, an Exhibition of 65 Graphic Works, The American Federation of Arts, New York

The Responsive Eye, The Museum of Modern Art, New York

Seven Americans, The Arkansas Art Center, Little Rock

Vibrations Eleven, Martha Jackson Gallery, New York

1966
Art of the United States, 1670–1966, The Whitney Museum of American Art, New York

The W. Hawkins Ferry Collection, The Detroit Institute of Arts

The First Flint International, Flint Institute of Arts, Michigan

Five Years: The Friends of the Corcoran, The Corcoran Gallery of Art, Washington, D.C.

Radius 5, Lafayette College, Easton, Pennsylvania

Seven Decades, 1895–1965, Cordier and Eckstrom Gallery, New York

Three Generations: Albers, Vasarely, Anuszkiewicz, The J. L. Hudson Gallery, Detroit

The White House Festival of the Arts, Washington, D.C.

1967
American Painting Now, United States Pavilion at Expo '67, Montreal, Canada (also shown at Institute of Contemporary Art, Boston)

The Benjamin Collection, a Loan Exhibition, Yale University Art Gallery, New Haven, Connecticut

Color Image and Form, The Detroit Institute of Arts

Focus on Light, The New Jersey State Museum, Trenton

Galerie der Spiegel, Cologne, West Germany

Geometric Art, The New Jersey State Museum, Trenton

1967 Annual Exhibition of Contemporary American Painting, The Whitney Museum of American Art, New York

The 1967 Pittsburgh International Exhibition of Contemporary Painting and Sculpture, Carnegie Institute, Pittsburgh

Selections from the Collection of Susan Morse Hilles, The Larry Aldrich Museum of Contemporary Art, Ridgefield, Connecticut

1968
The Bradley Collection, Milwaukee Art Center, Wisconsin

Dokumenta IV, Kassel, West Germany

Highlights of the 1967–1968 Art Season, The Larry Aldrich Museum of Contemporary Art, Ridgefield, Connecticut

Icon/Idea, Lafayette College, Easton, Pennsylvania

Paintings from The Albright-Knox Art Gallery, Buffalo, New York, The National Gallery of Art, Washington, D.C.

Plus by Minus, The Albright-Knox Art Gallery, Buffalo, New York

Signals in the 'Sixties, Honolulu Academy of Arts, Hawaii

The Square in Painting, The American Federation of Fine Arts, New York

1969
Contemporary Art—Acquisitions 1966–1969, The Albright-Knox Art Gallery, Buffalo, New York

Exposition–Position, Galerie Denise René, Paris

1969 Annual Exhibition, The Whitney Museum of American Art, New York

Prints and Posters from the U.S.A., U.S. Cultural Center, Tel Aviv, Israel

Sixteenth National Print Exhibition, The Brooklyn Museum, New York

1970
Contemporary American Art, 1870–1970 Centennial Exhibition, Indiana State University, Bloomington

How a Screen Print Is Made, The American Federation of Fine Arts, New York

The 1970 Pittsburgh International Exhibition of Contemporary Painting and Sculpture, Carnegie Institute, Pittsburgh

The Protean Century, 1870–1970, a Loan Exhibition from the Dartmouth College Collection, M. Knoedler, Inc., New York

1971
Anuszkiewicz—Fangor—Segal, Newark State College, Union, New Jersey

Anuszkiewicz—Segal, The New Jersey State College, Trenton

Highlights of the 1970–71 Art Season, The Larry Aldrich Museum of Contemporary Art, Ridgefield, Connecticut

Seventh Triennial—New Jersey Artists, Newark Museum, Newark, New Jersey

The Structure of Color, The Whitney Museum of American Art, New York

Works on Paper, The Art Institute of Chicago

1972
Color Painting, Mead Art Building, Amherst College, Amherst, Massachusetts

Friends of the Delaware Art Museum, Wilmington

Hall Gallery, Miami Beach, Florida

1972 Annual Exhibition, The Whitney Museum of American Art, New York

Recent Paintings and Sculpture, Munson-Williams-Proctor Institute, Utica, New York

1973
Anuszkiewicz—Stanczac, Mansfield Art Center, Mansfield, Ohio

1974
Dealer's Choice, The New York Cultural Center, New York

Opening Exhibition, Hirshhorn Museum and Sculpture Garden, Washington, D.C.

Twentieth-century American Painters, Andrew Crispo Gallery, New York

Twenty-fifth Anniversary Exhibition, Part II, Sidney Janis Gallery, New York

1975
Thirty-fourth Biennial of Contemporary American painting, The Corcoran Gallery of Art, Washington, D.C.

Pittsburgh Corporations Collect, Heinz Galleries, Carnegie Institute, Pittsburgh, Pennsylvania

The Growing Spectrum of American Art, Joslyn Art Museum, Omaha, Nebraska

Forms of Color, Akron Art Institute, Akron, Ohio

1976
Painting and Sculpture Today, Indianapolis Museum of Art, Indianapolis, Indiana

BIBLIOGRAPHY

BOOKS

Albers, Josef. *Interaction of Color* (rev. ed.). New Haven, Conn., and London: Yale University Press, 1975

Alloway, Lawrence. "Notes on Op Art." In *The New Art: A Critical Anthology* (Gregory Battcock, ed.), pp. 83–91. New York: E. P. Dutton & Co., 1966

Anuszkiewicz, Richard. "A Study in the Creation of Space with Life Drawing." M.F.A. thesis, Yale University, 1955

Arnason, H. H. *History of Modern Art: Painting, Sculpture, Architecture.* New York: Harry N. Abrams, [1968]

Arnheim, Rudolf. *Art and Visual Perception: A Psychology of the Creative Eye* (exp. and rev. ed.). Berkeley and Los Angeles: University of California Press, 1974

————— *Toward a Psychology of Art: Collected Essays.* Berkeley and Los Angeles: University of California Press, 1966

————— *Visual Thinking.* Berkeley and Los Angeles: University of California Press, 1969

Barrett, Cyril. *Op Art.* New York: The Viking Press, 1970

Birren, Faber. *History of Color in Painting: With New Principles of Color Expression.* New York: Reinhold Publishing Corporation, 1965

Boring, Edwin G. *Sensation and Perception in the History of Experimental Psychology.* New York: Appleton-Century-Crofts, 1942

Chevreul, Michel Eugène. *The Principles of Harmony and Contrast of Colors and Their Application to the Arts* (repr.). New York and London: Reinhold Publishing Corporation, 1967

Elsen, Albert E. *Purposes of Art: An Introduction to the History and Appreciation of Art* (2d ed.). New York and London: Holt, Rinehart and Winston, n.d. [1967]

Encyclopaedia Britannica, vol. I, p. 434. Chicago: Encyclopaedia Britannica, Inc., 1974

Encyclopedia of World Art, vol. X, cols. 204, 769. New York: McGraw-Hill, 1965

Fuller, R. Buckminster, and Robert Marks. *The Dymaxion World of Buckminster Fuller* (rev. ed.). Garden City, N.Y.: Anchor Books/Doubleday, 1973

Gibson, Eleanor J. *Principles of Perceptual Learning and Development.* New York: Appleton-Century-Crofts, 1969

Gibson, James J. *The Perception of the Visual World.* Boston and San Francisco: Houghton Mifflin Company, The Riverside Press, 1950

————— *The Senses Considered as Perceptual Systems.* Boston: Houghton Mifflin Company, 1966

Hunter, Sam. *La pittura americana del dopoguerra.* Milan: Fratelli Fabbri, 1970

————— and John Jacobus. *American Art of the Twentieth Century: Painting, Sculpture, Architecture.* New York: Harry N. Abrams, [1973]

Itten, Johannes. *The Art of Color: The Subjective Experience and Objective Rationale of Color* (Ernst van Haagen, trans.). New York and Melbourne: Van Nostrand Reinhold Company, 1961

Ivins, William M., Jr. *Art & Geometry: A Study in Space Intuitions.* Cambridge, Mass.: Harvard University Press, 1946; New York: Dover Publications, 1964 (repr.)

Knobler, Nathan. *The Visual Dialogue:*

An Introduction to the Appreciation of Art (2d ed.). New York: Holt, Rinehart and Winston, 1971

Koffka, K[urt]. *Principles of Gestalt Psychology.* New York: Harcourt, Brace and Company, 1935; A Harbinger Book (paperback), 1963

Luckiesh, M. *Visual Illusions: Their Causes, Characteristics and Applications* (new introd. by William H. Ittleson). New York: Dover Publications, 1965

Mellow, James A. "Art Explosion." In *The New York Times Encyclopedic Almanac 1970* (Seymour Kurz, ed.), pp. 629–30. New York: World Publishing Co., 1969

Mendelowitz, Daniel M. *A History of American Art* (2d ed.). New York: Holt, Rinehart and Winston, 1970

Ostwald, Wilhelm. *The Color Primer: A Basic Treatise on the Color System of Wilhelm Ostwald* (foreword and evaluation by Faber Birren, ed.). New York and Melbourne: Van Nostrand Reinhold Company, 1969 [original German ed., 1916]

Parola, Rene. *Optical Art: Theory and Practice.* New York and Amsterdam: Reinhold Book Corporation, 1969

Popper, Frank. *Origins and Development of Kinetic Art* (Stephen Bann, trans.). Greenwich, Conn.: New York Graphic Society, n.d.; London: Studio Vista, 1968

Rickey, George. *Constructivism: Origins and Evolution.* New York: George Braziller, 1967

Rood, Ogden N. *Modern Chromatics: Students' Text-Book of Color with Applications to Art and Industry* (including a facsimile of the first American ed. [New York: D. Appleton and Company, 1879]; preface, introduction and commentary notes by Faber Birren). New York and Melbourne: Van Nostrand Reinhold Company, 1973

Woody, Russell O., Jr. *Polymer Painting, and Related Techniques.* New York and Melbourne: Van Nostrand Reinhold Company, n.d.

PERIODICALS

Amaya, Mario. "Trays by Ten Artists," *Art in America*, vol. 59, January/February, 1971, pp. 48–57

Arnason, H. H. "The Precisionists: The New Geometry," *Art in America*, vol. 48, no. 3, 1960, pp. 54–61

Baro, Gene. "New York Exhibitions: A Gathering of Americans," *Arts Magazine*, vol. 37, September, 1963, pp. 28–33

B[enediki], M[ichael]. "Reviews and Previews," *Art News*, vol. 69, no. 10, February, 1971, p. 17

Bowness, Alan. "54/64 Painting and Sculpture of a Decade: The Gulbenkian Exhibition," *Studio International*, vol. 167, May 1964, pp. 190–95

B[uehr], W[endy]. "A Banner Year for Banners," *Horizon*, vol. 6, Spring 1964, pp. 60–65.

B[urrows], C[arlyle]. "Art Exhibition Notes: 'Scientific' Designs," *New York Herald Tribune*, Apr. 8, 1961, p. 5

Canaday, John. "American Drawings: Or, the Sad Case of the Hidden Virtues," *The New York Times*, Oct. 25, 1964, sec. 2, p. 13

———— "Americans Once More," *The New York Times*, May 26, 1963, sec. 2, p. 11

————"Art: Eakins in New York at Last," *The New York Times*, Sept. 27, 1970, sec. 2, p. 23

———— "Art: Fifteen Exhibit at Modern," *The New York Times*, May 22, 1963, p. 38

———— "Art: Optics Are the Stalk of the Town," *The New York Times*, Jan. 30, 1965, p. 24

———— "Art That Pulses, Quivers and Fascinates," *The New York Times Magazine*, Feb. 21, 1965, pp. 12–13, 55–57, 59

———— "The Responsive Eye: Three Cheers and High Hopes," Feb. 28, 1965, sec. 2, p. 19

———— "Richard Anuszkiewicz: It's Baffling," *The New York Times*, Apr. 5, 1969, p. 23

Chapin, Louis. "New York Reviews," *Art News*, vol. 74, no. 5, May, 1975, pp. 98–99

Coates, Robert M. "The Art Galleries: 'Op'," *The New Yorker*, vol. 41, Mar. 27, 1965, pp. 161–64, 167

Doty, Robert. "Richard Anuszkiewicz," *Museum News*, vol. 48, January, 1970, pp. 11–12

Eye: Magazine of the Yale Arts Association, no. 2, 1968

Genauer, Emily. "138 Pictures by Living Artists: American Art Survey: '65 Edition at Whitney," *New York Herald Tribune*, Dec. 8, 1965, p. 29

———— "The Wizards of Op," *New York: The Sunday Herald Tribune Magazine*, Feb. 21, 1965, pp. 30, 32, 58

Getlein, Frank. "Biennial Show at the Corcoran," *Washington Sunday Star*, Feb. 28, 1965

Glueck, Grace. "Art Notes: Blues and Greens on Reds," *The New York Times*, Feb. 21, 1965, sec. 2, p. 19

————"Out of St. Cyr: Furrier to the Art World," *The New York Times Magazine*, Oct. 2, 1966, pp. 39, 135–39

Gray, Cleve. "Ceramics by Twelve Artists," *Art in America*, vol. 52, December, 1964, pp. 27–41

Gruen, John. "Art: 'Op' Pops and Their Opsprings," *New York: The Sunday Herald Tribune Magazine*, Feb. 7, 1965, p. 32.

———— "Pop Goes the Easel," *New York Herald Tribune*, May 26, 1963, sec. 4, p. 6

Jacobs, Jay. "Pertinent & Impertinent: Publisher," *TheARTgallery Magazine*, vol. 13, October, 1969

———— "Portrait of the Artist—Richard Anuszkiewicz," *TheARTgallery Magazine*, vol. 14, March, 1971, pp. 21–35

Jameson, Dorothea, and Leo M. Hurvich. "From Contrast to Assimilation: in Art and in the Eye," *Leonardo*, vol 8, 1975, pp. 125–131

Jersey City Awake: A City in Transition (pamphlet), New Jersey State Council on the Arts, Trenton, N.J., n.d. [1972]

Karshan, Donald H. "Graphics '70: Richard Anuszkiewicz," *Art in America*, vol. 58, March/April, 1970, pp. 56–59

Kramer, Hilton. "Art: Clashing Values of Two Generations," *The New York Times*, Nov. 6, 1965, p. 26

Krauss, Rosalind. "Afterthoughts on 'Op'," *Art International*, vol. 9, June, 1965, pp. 75–76

K[urtz], S[tephen] A. "Reviews and Previews," *Art News*, vol. 68, no. 2, April, 1969, p. 8

Lunde, Karl. "Richard Anuszkiewicz," *Arts Magazine*, February, 1975, pp. 56–57

Lynes, Russell. "The Mesh Canvas," *Art in America*, vol. 56, May/June, 1968, pp. 28–49

Mayor, A. Hyatt. "Painters' Playing Cards," *Art in America*, vol. 51, no. 2, 1963, pp. 39–42

Milwaukee Art Center Annual Report 1969, May, 1970

Morris, Bernardine. "Anuszkiewicz Sets Legs into Motion," *The New York Times*, May 29, 1965, p. 15

Neumann, Eckhard. "Op-Art," *Kunst*, vol. 5, February/April, 1965, pp. 36–41

"O Say Can You See," *Newsweek*, vol. 65, Jan. 11, 1965, p. 78

O'Doherty, Brian. "Art: 'The Classic Spirit'," *The New York Times*, Feb. 4, 1964, p. 66

"Op: Adventure Without Danger," *Newsweek*, vol. 65, Mar. 1, 1965, pp. 82–83

"Op Art: Pictures That Attack the Eye," *Time*, vol. 84, Oct. 23, 1964, pp. 78–86

Ortman, George. "Artists' Games," *Art in America*, vol. 57, November/December, 1969, pp. 69–77

"Painting and Sculpture Acquisitions, 1960," *The Museum of Modern Art Bulletin*, vol. 28, nos. 2–4, pp. 5, 54–55

P[erreault], J[ohn]. "Reviews and Previews," *Art News*, vol. 66, no. 6, October, 1967, p. 12

Preston, Stuart. "Adventures and Renewals: Slight of Eye," *The New York Times*, Apr. 2, 1961, sec. 2, p. 16

——— "'Les Animaliers' Stage Comeback," *The New York Times*, Mar. 4, 1963, p. 9

——— "Art: American Geometric Abstraction," *The New York Times*, Mar. 21, 1962, p. 36

——— "Connecticut Sets the Pace," *The New York Times*, July 5, 1964, sec. 2, p. 15

"Recent Acquisition," *Virginia Museum Bulletin*, vol. 31, September, 1970, n.p.

"Recent Acquisitions," *City Art Museum of Saint Louis Bulletin*, vol. 2, May/June, 1966, cover and pp. 1–3

"Richard Anuszkiewicz: Primary Contrast," *Currier Gallery of Art Bulletin*, July/August, 1966

Rickey, George. "Scandale de Succès," *Art International*, vol. 9, May, 1965, pp. 16–23

Roditi, Edouard. "International Reports: Paris: A Theology of Hard-Edge," *Arts Magazine*, vol. 38, December, 1963, pp. 34–37

Rose, Barbara. "New York Letter," *Art International*, vol. 7, Apr. 25, 1963, pp. 57–60

Rosenberg, Harold. "The Art Galleries: Black and Pistachio," *The New Yorker*, vol. 39, June 15, 1964, p. 84 ff.

——— "From Pollock to Pop: Twenty Years of Painting and Sculpture," *Holiday*, vol. 39, March, 1966, pp. 96–105, 136–38, 140

Rosenthal, Nan. "Brightening the Scene —List Art Posters," *Art in America*, vol. 53, April, 1965, pp. 56–65

Russell, John. "Collector: Larry Aldrich," *Art in America*, vol. 57, January/February, 1969, pp. 56–65

Seitz, William C. "The New Perceptual Art," *Vogue*, vol. 145, Feb. 15, 1965, pp. 78–80, 142–43

Sheppard, Eugenia. "Inside Fashion: Pop Furs May Be Popular," *New York Herald Tribune*, June 9, 1963, sec. 1, p. 28

Shirey, David L. "Reviews and Previews," *Art News*, vol. 72, no. 2, February, 1973, pp. 82–83

"Simple Form, Simple Color," *Time*, vol. 82, July 19, 1963, pp. 56–57, 59

Slate, Joseph. "So Hard to Look at: An Interview with Richard Anuszkiewicz," *Contempora*, May/June, 1970

Smith, Miles A. "Pop Art Losing Its Shock Appeal?" *Daily American*, July 4, 1963

Taylor, Brie. "Towards a Plastic Revolution," *Art News*, vol. 63, March, 1964, pp. 46–49, 62–63

Tillim, Sidney. "Optical Art: Pending or Ending?" *Arts Magazine*, vol. 39, January, 1965, pp. 16–23

Todd, Anne G. "'Op' Show Is Fascinating," *Seattle Times*, July 18, 1965

Willard, Charlotte. "Alfred Barr: New York Forecaster of Trends in Modern Art," *Look*, vol. 27, Mar. 26, 1963, pp. 86–88

——— "Art Centers: New York: Dealers-Eye View," *Art in America*, vol. 52, April, 1964, p. 120 ff.

——— "Drawing Today," *Art in America*, vol. 52, October, 1964, pp. 49–67

EXHIBITION CATALOGUES

Albright-Knox Art Gallery, Buffalo, N.Y. *Art Today: Kinetic and Optic*, 1965

——— *Contemporary Art—Acquisitions 1962–1965*, 1965

——— *Contemporary Art—Acquisitions 1966–1969*, 1969

——— *Plus by Minus: Today's Half-Century* (text by Douglas MacAgy), 1968

The American Federation of Arts, New York. *How a Screen Print Is Made* (introd. by H. L. C. Jaffe; text by Eric Vietze), 1970

——— *Pop and Op* (foreword by George Weissman; introd. by Max Kozloff; sponsored by Philip Morris, Inc.), n.p., [1965?]

——— *The Square in Painting* (selected by Richard Anuszkiewicz), 1969

Andrew Crispo Gallery, New York. *Rich-*

ard Anuszkiewicz: Recent Paintings, 1975

The Arkansas Arts Center, Little Rock. Seven Americans, 1965

The Art Institute of Chicago. Sixty-seventh Annual American Exhibition: Directions in American Painting, 1964

Brandeis University, Poses Institute of Fine Arts, Waltham, Mass. New Directions in American Painting, 1963

The Brooklyn Museum, Brooklyn, N.Y. Sixteenth National Print Exhibition: Two Decades of American Prints 1947–1968 (introd. by Una E. Johnson), 1968

The Butler Institute of American Art, Youngstown, Ohio. Thirtieth Annual Midyear Show, [1965]

Carnegie Institute Museum of Art, Pittsburgh, Penn. The 1964 Pittsburgh International: Exhibition of Contemporary Painting and Sculpture (foreword by Gustave von Groschwitz), 1964

——— The 1967 Pittsburgh International Exhibition of Contemporary Painting and Sculpture (foreword by Gustave von Groschwitz), 1967

——— The 1970 Pittsburgh International Exhibition of Contemporary Art (introd. by Leon Anthony Arkus), 1970

The Corcoran Gallery of Art, Washington, D.C. Five Years: The Friends of the Corcoran, "The Contemporary Spirit" (preface by Hermann Warner Williams, Jr.), 1966

——— The Twenty-ninth Biennial Exhibition of Contemporary American Painting (introd. by Hermann Warner Williams, Jr.), 1965

Dartmouth College Arts Council, Dartmouth College, Hanover, N.H. The Protean Century 1870–1970: A Loan Exhibition from The Dartmouth College Collection, Alumni and Friends of the College, 1970

DeCordova Museum, Lincoln, Mass. New Experiments in Art, 1963

——— Paintings by Richard Anuszkiewicz (foreword by Carlo M. Lamagna), 1972

The Detroit Institute of Arts. The W. Hawkins Ferry Collection (introd. by Joshua C. Taylor), 1966

Ferdinand Roten Galleries, Inc., Baltimore, Md. Catalogue No. 12, 1970

Finch College Museum of Art, New York, The Josephine and Phillip A. Bruno Collection, 1965

Flint Institute of Arts, Flint, Mich. The First Flint Invitational: An Exhibition of Contemporary Painting and Sculpture (foreword by G. Stuart Hodge), 1966

Galerie Denise René, Paris. Exposition-Position, 1969

——— Mouvement 2, 1964

Honolulu Academy of Arts. Signals in the 'Sixties (foreword by James W. Foster, Jr.; introd. by James Johnson Sweeney), 1968

Hudson Company, The J. L., Detroit. Three Generations: Albers, Vasarely, Anuszkiewicz, 1966

Illinois, University of, Urbana, College of Fine and Applied Arts, Krannert Art Museum. Contemporary American Painting and Sculpture (foreword by C. V. Donovan; text by Allen S. Weller), University of Illinois Press, 1961

——— Eleventh Exhibition of Contemporary American Painting and Sculpture, 1963 (foreword by C. V. Donovan; introd. by Allen S. Weller), University of Illinois Press, 1963

Indiana State University, Bloomington, Ind., Turman Art Gallery. Contemporary American Art, 1870–1970 Centennial Exhibition, 1970

Institute of Contemporary Art, Boston. American Painting Now (introd. by Alan Solomon), 1967

Kent State University, Kent, Ohio, Van

Deusen Gallery. Fifteen Paintings/Anuszkiewicz, 1968

Lafayette College, Easton, Pa. Icon/Idea: Josef Albers, Richard Anuszkiewicz, Clarence Carter, Paul Jenkins, George Ortman (introd. by James A. Michener), 1968

——— Radius 5 (foreword by James A. Michener), 1966

The Larry Aldrich Museum [of Contemporary Art], Ridgefield, Conn. Art of the 50's and 60's: Selections from the Richard Brown Baker Collection (statements by Larry Aldrich and Richard Brown Baker), 1965

——— Highlights of the 1967–68 Art Season, 1968

——— "Old Hundred," Selections from the Larry Aldrich Contemporary Collection, 1951–1964, 1964

——— Selections from the Collection of Susan Morse Hilles (introd. by Larry Aldrich; statement by Susan Morse Hilles), [1967]

Lyman Allyn Museum, New London, Conn. Selections from the Collection of Susan Morse Hilles (foreword by Edgar deN. Mayhew), [1967]

Martha Jackson Gallery, New York. Vibrations Eleven, 1965

The Metropolitan Museum of Art, New York. New York Painting and Sculpture: 1940–1970 (text by Henry Geldzahler), E. P. Dutton & Co., 1969

Michigan, University of, Ann Arbor, Mich., Museum of Art. The New Formalists. Contemporary American Paintings for Purchase Considerations, 1964

Milwaukee Art Center. The Collection of Mrs. Harry Lynde Bradley (introd. by Tracy Atkinson), 1968

The Museum of Modern Art, New York. Americans 1963 (edited by Dorothy C. Miller, with statements by the artists and others), 1963

——— The Responsive Eye (text by William C. Seitz), 1965

————— The Sidney and Harriet Janis Collection: A Gift to The Museum of Modern Art (preface by Alfred H. Barr, Jr.), 1968

National Gallery of Art, Washington, D.C. Paintings from the Albright-Knox Art Gallery, Buffalo, New York (foreword by John Walker), 1968

The New Jersey State Museum, Trenton, N.J. Focus on Light (organized by Richard Bellamy, Lucy R. Lippard, and Leah P. Sloshberg; foreword by Edward A. Ring; essay by Lucy R. Lippard), 1967

————— Geometric Art: An Exhibition of Paintings and Constructions by Fourteen Contemporary New Jersey Artists (foreword by Leah Phyfer Sloshberg), 1967

————— Paintings by Richard Anuszkiewicz/Sculpture by George Segal (foreword by Leah Sloshberg; introd. by Zoltan Buki), 1971

New York World's Fair, 1964, Pavilion of Fine Arts. American Art Today (presented by Long Island Arts Center, Inc.), n.p., n.d.

Public Education Association, New York. Seven Decades 1895–1965: Cross Currents in Modern Art (text by Peter Selz), 1966

Sidney Janis Gallery, New York. Anuszkiewicz, 1971

————— Anuszkiewicz: New Paintings, 1969

————— New Paintings by Anuszkiewicz, 1965

————— New Paintings by Anuszkiewicz, 1967

————— Pop and Op, 1964

Silvermine Guild of Artists, New Canaan, Conn. Silvermine Guild of Artists Fifteenth Annual New England Exhibition, 1964

Tel Aviv, Museum of. Art et mouvement—art optique et cinétique (organized in collaboration with the Galerie Denise René, Paris), 1965

Tel Aviv, United States Cultural Center. Prints and Posters from the U.S.A. (foreword by John D. Congleton), 1969

Texas, The University of, Austin, The University Art Museum. 1 + 1 = 3: An Exhibition of Retinal and Perceptual Art (introd. by Donald B. Goodall; statement by Vincent Mariani), n.d.

United States Information Service. Anuszkiewicz, [Washington, D.C.], 1974

Washington Gallery of Modern Art, Washington, D.C. The Formalists, 1963

Whitney Museum of American Art, New York. Annual Exhibition 1963: Contemporary American Painting, [1963]

————— Annual Exhibition 1966: Contemporary Sculpture and Prints, [1966]

————— Art of the United States: 1670–1966, 2 vols. (text by Lloyd Goodrich), 1966

————— A Decade of American Drawings 1955–1965: Eighth Exhibition Sponsored by the Friends (foreword by Donald M. Blinken), [1965]

————— Geometric Abstraction in America: Fifth Loan Exhibition, Friends of the Whitney Museum of American Art (essay by John Gordon), 1962

————— 1965 Annual Exhibition of Contemporary American Painting, [1965]

————— 1967 Annual Exhibition of Contemporary Painting, [1967]

————— 1969 Annual Exhibition, Contemporary American Painting, [1969]

————— 1972 Annual Exhibition, Contemporary American Painting, [1972]

————— The Structure of Color (text by Marcia Tucker), 1971

Yale University Art Gallery, New Haven, Conn. The Helen W. and Robert M. Benjamin Collection: A Loan Exhibition (introd. by Lloyd Goodrich), 1967

INDEX

Plate numbers in *italic* type indicate colorplates.

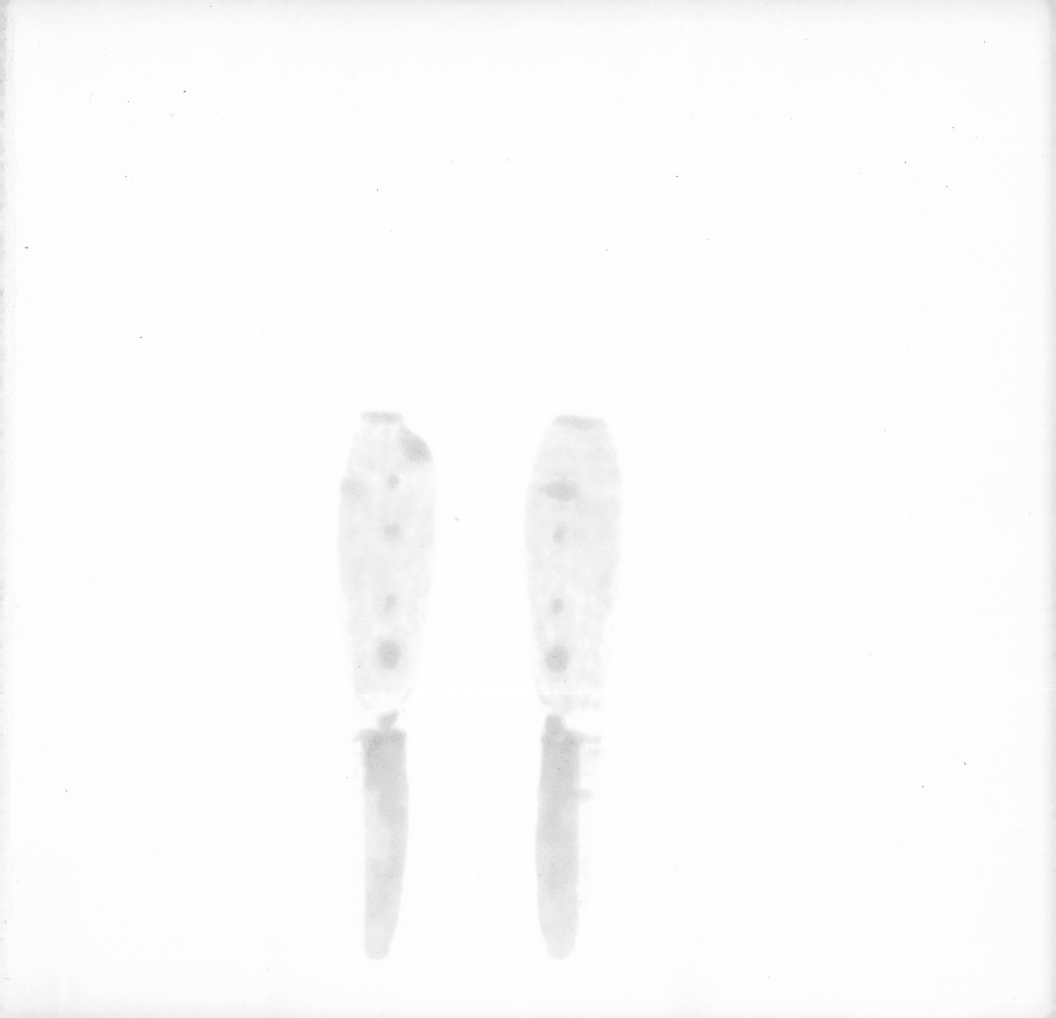